SIR HALLEY STEWART TRUST: LECTURES

Volume 1

THE ORDEAL OF THIS GENERATION

THE ORDEAL OF THIS GENERATION

The War, the League and the Future

GILBERT MURRAY

LONDON AND NEW YORK

First published in 1929 by George Allen & Unwin Ltd.

This edition first published in 2025
by Routledge
4 Park Square, Milton Park, Abingdon, Oxon OX14 4RN

and by Routledge
605 Third Avenue, New York, NY 10158

Routledge is an imprint of the Taylor & Francis Group, an informa business

© 1929 Sir Halley Stewart Trust

All rights reserved. No part of this book may be reprinted or reproduced or utilised in any form or by any electronic, mechanical, or other means, now known or hereafter invented, including photocopying and recording, or in any information storage or retrieval system, without permission in writing from the publishers.

Trademark notice: Product or corporate names may be trademarks or registered trademarks, and are used only for identification and explanation without intent to infringe.

British Library Cataloguing in Publication Data
A catalogue record for this book is available from the British Library

ISBN: 978-1-032-88942-9 (Set)
ISBN: 978-1-032-80719-5 (Volume 1) (hbk)
ISBN: 978-1-032-80722-5 (Volume 1) (pbk)
ISBN: 978-1-003-49826-1 (Volume 1) (ebk)

DOI: 10.4324/9781003498261

Publisher's Note
The publisher has gone to great lengths to ensure the quality of this reprint but points out that some imperfections in the original copies may be apparent.

Disclaimer
The publisher has made every effort to trace copyright holders and would welcome correspondence from those they have been unable to trace.

This book is a re-issue originally published in 1929. The language used and views portrayed are a reflection of its era and no offence is meant by the Publishers to any reader by this re-publication.

THE HALLEY STEWART TRUST

FOUNDED 15TH DECEMBER 1924
FOR RESEARCH TOWARDS THE CHRISTIAN IDEAL IN ALL SOCIAL LIFE.

TRUSTEES:
HALLEY STEWART, J.P., *Chairman.*
PERCY MALCOLM STEWART, O.B.E., J.P.
PERCY ALDEN, M.A.
BERNARD HALLEY STEWART, M.A., M.D.
SIDNEY MALCOLM BERRY, M.A., D.D.
THOMAS HYWEL HUGHES, M.A., D.LIT., D.D.
ALBERT PEEL, M.A., D.LIT.
HAROLD BEAUMONT SHEPHEARD, M.A.
STANLEY UNWIN.

The objects of the Trust are *in general*:

To advance religion; to advance education; to relieve poverty; to promote other Charitable purposes beneficial to the community, and *in particular*:

1. To assist in the discovery of the best means by which "the mind of Christ" may be applied to extending the Kingdom of God by the prevention and removal of human misery;
2. To assist in the study of our Lord's life and teaching in their explicit and implicit application to the social relationships of man;
3. To express the mind of Christ in the realization of the Kingdom of God upon earth and in a national and a world-wide brotherhood;

For example:

For every Individual, by furthering such favourable opportunities of education, service, and leisure as shall enable him or her most perfectly to develop the body, mind, and spirit:

In all Social Life, whether domestic, industrial, or national, by securing a just environment, and

In International Relationships, by fostering good will between all races, tribes, peoples, and nations so as to secure the fulfilment of the hope of "peace on earth";

4. To provide fees for a Lecture or Lectures annually and prizes for essays or other written compositions, and to pay for their publication and distribution;
5. To provide, maintain, and assist Lectures and Research work in Social, Economic, Psychological, Medical, Surgical, or Educational subjects;
6. To make grants to Libraries;
7. To assist publications exclusively connected with the objects of the Trust (not being newspapers or exclusively denominational);
8. To make grants to and co-operate with Societies, Organizations, and Persons engaged in the furtherance of Charitable objects similar to the objects of the Trust;
9. To use the foregoing and any such other methods, whether of a like nature or not, as are lawful and reasonable and appropriate for the furtherance of the objects of the Trust.

The income of the Trust may not be used for dogmatic theological or ecclesiastical purposes other than the cult of the Science of God as manifest in man in the Son of Man in the person and teaching of Our Lord, "The Word of God", Who "liveth and abideth for ever".

HALLEY STEWART LECTURES, 1928

THE ORDEAL OF THIS GENERATION

THE WAR, THE LEAGUE & THE FUTURE

BY

GILBERT MURRAY, LL.D., D.Litt., F.B.A

LONDON
GEORGE ALLEN & UNWIN LTD
MUSEUM STREET

FIRST PUBLISHED IN 1929

All rights reserved

PRINTED IN GREAT BRITAIN BY
UNWIN BROTHERS LTD., WOKING

PACIS PROPUGNATORIBUS DOMESTICAE EXTERNAEQUE
BARBARAE ET LAURENTIO HAMMOND
VETERIS MEMOR AMICITIAE
LIBELLUM DEDICO

PREFACE

PROFOUND changes, political, social, economic and intellectual, have taken place during the last fifty years in the environment of civilized man, and it is still doubtful whether or no he will succeed in understanding them and adapting himself to meet them. That is the "ordeal" which forms the subject of these lectures, delivered in the autumn of 1928 under the auspices of the Halley Stewart Trust. My approach to the problem is no doubt influenced both by my work for the League of Nations Union and my membership of that organ of the League which bears the name of C.I.C., or Committee of Intellectual Co-operation. I should like also to believe that the book showed some effects of the sympathy and the inspiring example of Mr. Halley Stewart himself.

I have ventured to include as a not irrelevant addition an earlier lecture dealing with the Future of the British Empire in relation to the League of Nations.

It is almost superfluous to say how great a debt I owe to the annual *Survey* published by the British Institute of International Affairs.

G. M.

CONTENTS

	PAGE
PREFACE	9

I

PEACE AND STRIFE AS ELEMENTS IN LIFE: THE IDEAL OF "UNHINDERED ACTIVITY" 13

Strife a permanent element in life, but War not. Peace as "unimpeded activity": the service of Civilization.

II

THE CIVILIZATION OF THE NINETEENTH CENTURY 41

Its greatness and the flaw which led to its collapse. Domestic order and international anarchy.

III

THE FELT NEED 67

The effort to correct this flaw has led naturally to the three fundamental principles of the Covenant: Conference, Law, Sanctions.

IV

THE WORLD INSIDE THE COVENANT 99

The imperfections of the document, the failure of nations and Governments to live up to it.

V

THE WORLD OUTSIDE THE COVENANT 135

Problems and Regions not covered by the Covenant; the consequent dangers to civilization.

VI

FROM CHAOS TO COSMOS 169

The building of a new Order and the need of Intellectual Co-operation.

VII

THE SPECIAL PROBLEMS OF THE BRITISH EMPIRE IN RELATION TO THE LEAGUE OF NATIONS 202

THE ORDEAL OF THIS GENERATION

I

PEACE AND STRIFE AS ELEMENTS IN LIFE: THE IDEAL OF "UNHINDERED ACTIVITY"

WE hear much of Peace as an ideal. Most of my readers will be friends of peace, pleaders of the cause of peace; always in controversy, as it were, with people whom we call militarists, and who in return call us other names. And I think we are often somewhat puzzled to find how little impression our reasoning makes upon the unconverted, and how much of the enthusiasm of the world is still against us. One could perhaps understand the problem better if our opponents talked more; but we do most of the talking. They generally remain inarticulate, and are content with disbelieving and rather despising us. It is worth while, therefore, if we allow ourselves to make an ideal of peace, to think carefully what we mean by the word.

To a soldier worn out by extreme labour and suffering, Peace means, no doubt, a rest and a cessation, a time in which he shall cease fighting and being fought against, shall do nothing and have nothing done to him; and that thought may well sum up for the moment the extreme goal of his desires. But of course after a time his desire will change; he will be sick of peace and demand action, adventure, danger. Perpetual peace, as the well-known story in Kant's treatise tells us, is a thing that man may find in the churchyard, but not before. "It is a dream," says another authority, "and not a pleasant dream"; and as long as we regard peace purely as a negative thing, a time of mere repose during which we neither strive ourselves nor are striven against, the criticism seems to me perfectly true. The old irritating phrases, descended from a social state quite different from ours, which speak of a nation "fusting" or "rotting" in prolonged peace, would have some sense in them if by Peace we really meant a negative thing, a mere respite from action and feeling.

Life is obviously a rhythm of waking and sleeping, toil and rest, strife and peace. Nor is it by any means clear that the first element in the alternation is bad and the second good. It may sometimes be true that we do a hard day's work in order to get a good night's rest; but it is much more that we want a good night's rest for the sake of the work to be done to-morrow. Aristotle, indeed, says, in words that are often quoted: "We toil for the sake of leisure, we make war for the sake of peace." But observe he here makes Peace parallel to Leisure, and leisure, of course, is not idleness. It is the time in which you are free to do the things that you really want to do, as distinguished from those which you are compelled to do. We strive, really, not for the sake of mere rest or peace, but in order to be free to strive better for the objects that we really desire.

Thus, we must grant to the militarist that strife has at least as great a part in life as the opposite.

But the truth seems to be a little harsher than this. If the pacifist wants to see the truth, he must face the essential tragedy of life. Biologically the whole animal creation, or at any rate all the carnivorous part of it, kills in order to live. Man, of course, also kills for the pleasure of killing, and might possibly cure himself of that ferocious taste. But any notion of a peace which should free the human race or any fragment of it from the daily continual habit of killing in order to live would be the shallowest philosophy or the wildest dream. We are always killing. And it is mere sluggishness of imagination which makes us sometimes forget the fact because the killing, in civilized cities at any rate, is hidden away like other messy things and performed by special classes of people. We must not be like a child in a nursery who is taught that it would be unkind to kill a wasp; he must sit still and consume his bovril and veal cutlets. This constant fighting and killing is one of the primary and fundamental facts of life, which must be realized if we are to understand any moral problems. Let me try to illustrate it by a parallel.

About the beginning of this century, in the time of the Young Turks, it was decided by the

Turkish Government that the pariah dogs which filled the streets of Constantinople must be removed. To kill them would have been repugnant to Turkish feeling; so the dogs were collected in some thousands, put on board ship and deported to an uninhabited island in the Sea of Marmora. There was nothing much to eat on the island; only a few rats, rabbits, and the like. About water I do not know. The hungry dogs first ate the other animals, and then one another. Then they starved and fought and died until after a time, I am told, the howling ceased. They might, of course, have been put on an island where there was a larger supply of small animals to eat and water to drink, but fundamentally the situation would have been the same. And it is the situation of practically the whole animal world; we all live by eating other animals or else by eating their food. Life is not based on peace: it is based on an unrelenting murderous struggle. It is difficult to conceive any scheme of creation which, judged by human standards, would be much more hideous.

And yet there is an element we have left out. I was told by my informant that naturally some of the dogs had puppies, and naturally the other dogs, especially the male dogs, tried to eat them first. It seemed such an easy way of getting food. Yet it was not, because of the mothers. The pariah bitch fought like a tigress to defend her puppies, and, fighting against odds, died for them. An element of love, of love and sacrifice, love that will die to save its object, is there present, a plain biological fact and necessity, in the midst of the struggle for life. One can go further. It has often been pointed out, and particularly by the late Prince Kropotkin in his book *Mutual Aid*, that the law Kill-to-live, though never entirely abrogated, becomes increasingly suffused and penetrated by another: Co-operate-to-live. The whole herd or flock acts as one in the interest of all; and such co-operation inevitably involves from time to time, not a struggle of all against all, but an actual sacrifice of self by the individual for the sake of the whole, or for the sake of other individuals. We are gregarious animals. And if such animals cannot live without killing, it is also true that they cannot live without loving one another and sacrificing themselves for one another. With increasing intelligence there is built up a social order. The striving of the herd or flock as a whole becomes to an increasing extent beneficent rather than destructive; within the flock almost entirely beneficent, and even towards those outside less indiscriminately hostile. This is the upward road of civilization. In the conscious life of a modern soldier, I suppose, the actual killing of the enemy plays a very small part compared with the regular routine of labour, discipline, co-operation, and the occasional risk of life and limb in supporting other troops in exposed positions or rescuing wounded companions. And one can well imagine it would be the same in any individual member of a pack of wolves or hunting dogs. The statement "God is Love", if applied to the general condition of the whole animal world, would seem to me a most grievous paradox. Love is certainly not the obvious characteristic of the struggle for life. But the phrase has truth in it and, one cannot help suspecting, very profound truth, if we take it as meaning that in a world which at first seems to be nothing but a universal murderous struggle there is, undeniable and inevitable, this element of Love which works like leaven transforming the whole mass, changing it, to say the least, from a sheer horror into a mystery. It provides, not indeed a solution, but a hope. But observe, so far we have not found peace, nor at all confuted the militarist. We have found two forms of strife, one based on self-protection and the other on Love.

We spoke of a rhythm in life, a rhythm of waking and sleeping, of toil and rest: more metaphorically perhaps we can speak of a rhythm of War and Peace, or Repulsion and Attraction. In one half of the rhythm you have always Strife—not, of course, necessarily hatred or even anger, but some striving against opposition, some conflict. Strife, in the strict sense of striving or conflict, is integral in life. You cannot fully have life without it. And it is a well-established principle of education that only by striving and conflict do you build up character, or achieve any improvement moral or physical. If Peace is to mean repose, or an absence of effort and striving, we certainly do not want it perpetual. It is a rather dangerous drug, a thing to be taken in very small doses. For we must face the fact not merely that some things are so good that we are justified in fighting for them, but that fighting in itself seems to be good. There is an old puzzle about the value of evolution, a puzzle much older than the theory of Evolution itself. What good can it ultimately be if, in the process of development, the deer grows faster and faster so as to escape from the lion, while at the same time the lion grows stronger and more cunning so as to catch the deer? Would it not have been just as good if they had both stayed as they were at first? It is an old question, and the ancient Stoics had an answer to it. "True," they said, "it does not matter a bit in the eyes of God that a deer should run twenty miles an hour instead of ten, or that a lion, able at first to catch such and such a percentage of ten-milers, should learn in the course of generations to catch an equal number of twenty-milers: neither fact matters at all. But what does matter is that the deer, and the lion also, should do whatever it has to do as well as it can. A deer or lion or worm can do its duty or fail to do it, just as a man can." The Stoics, as we all know, carried the principle consistently throughout their theory of morals. A doctor labours self-sacrificingly to deal with a pestilence, a good governor improves the prosperity of his people; yet it matters not at all in the eyes of God whether so many persons died of the pestilence in the year 1900 or of old age in the year 1920; whether the average income of the peasants under the good governor amounts to so many shillings a week or to half as much again;

the one thing that does matter is that the doctor should do his best, the governor do his best, and each go on doing his best though he die for it. It is the striving itself, the effort and the will-power, that make the only true element of value for these philosophers, and I think that the instinctive feeling of most people, before they begin to argue, largely agrees with them. It is the story of pluck or self-sacrifice that thrills the average man or child: the cause for which it is shown, or the result which it actually brings about, comes as an appendix to the story, sometimes interesting and sometimes not. Of course, it is perfectly true that in the eyes of a thoughtful person any strife becomes nobler the less there is in it of hatred, the more of co-operation or sacrifice for others, the more beneficent the end striven for. Yet it is curious to see how, both in romance and in newspaper stories, a pirate who fights well and dies game is more sure of sympathy than, say, a posse of armed policemen who shoot him down. We try to hold up to boys and girls the heroic missionary, the skilful doctor who faces risks in the practice of his art, even the strenuous and intelligent philanthropist; but, except where an incidental fight or mortal danger happens to come into the story, they have all a very poor chance against a soldier. Speakers for the League of Nations know only too well that if you show on a lantern slide two alternative ways of settling an international dispute—either by a cavalry charge with horses plunging and men sabring one another or falling dead under the hoofs, or by a conference of rather plain and bald old gentlemen reading papers to one another round a table—practically every young boy and girl in the room is secretly in favour of the cavalry charge. It is not that they want to kill, but they want to face death and peril. They want to put forth for one great moment the extreme effort in mind and body of which they are capable. They want to do it for others, for their country, for some great unspecified cause, so that if they live those whom they have saved will adore them, and if they die multitudes bless their memory. *Dulce et decorum est pro patria mori:* of course, it is *decorum*, honourable, to die for one's country. That we all know. But the poet says more than that. He says it is "sweet". Evidently, I think, he knew human nature.

We must realize the nobility of this ideal that we are setting out to correct, or we shall never make ourselves understood by those whom we seek to convert. The fighting man, the man who faces death for others or even for himself alone, makes an appeal to human instincts that are deep and not shallow. In all romance the soldier is above the merchant; and it is in romance that human instincts find their freest expression. But not only that. In real life the fighting races seem to have a way of winning general respect which is denied to those who have lost the power of fighting. I am told that at Hampton College, where Red Indians and negroes are educated together, the negroes mostly do better than the Indians at intellectual work, at debating societies, and even in games. Yet the Indians constitute a sort of aristocracy. Americans, who regard a dash of negro blood with consternation, are rather pleased than otherwise to be descended from a Red Indian. If we ask why, the reason seems to be that the Indians were fighters. The negro race submitted to slavery while the Indian fought to the death rather than submit.

When the Turks conquered the Armenians, they gave them the choice between two things: they might keep their religion, but if so they must give up their arms; or they might keep their arms, but if so they must give up their religion. The Armenians, passionately devoted to their religion, gave up their arms. They became in a sense a nation of martyrs, and one must never forget the fineness of their religious record; but, having lost their arms, they lost most of the military virtues, they depended for their safety more and more on submission and cunning, and became one of the most unpopular nations in the Near East.

When the Turks conquered the Albanians, they offered them the same choice. Now the Albanians set some store, of course, by their religion, but they could not quite put it in the same rank as their guns. They apostatized but kept their arms, and, though not remarkable for the civil or Christian virtues, are celebrated for their courage and sense of honour. When a friend of mine, engaged in Balkan Relief, had to send a large sum of money by hand over the Macedonian mountains and did not know how to find a messenger honest enough and bold enough to carry it, he was advised to engage an Albanian brigand. The brigand faced all the necessary dangers, paid over every penny, and reported again on the right day. That was, ultimately, because his ancestors had preferred their arms to their religion. Arms had saved them.

That is the case for militarism, as I understand it. It is a case which, to use the words of the philosopher William James, "must be listened to and respected. One cannot meet it effectively by mere counter-insistence on war's expensiveness and horror. The horror makes the thrill. And when the question is of getting the extremest and supremest out of human nature, talk of expense sounds ignominious. . . . The military party denies neither the bestiality of war nor the horror nor the expense; it only says that these things tell but half the story. It only says that war is worth them; that, taking human nature as a whole, its wars are its best protection against its weaker and more cowardly self, and that mankind cannot afford to adopt a peace economy".

Let us squarely face that contention. For if it is really true that the man who fights is apt to be morally superior all round to the man who does not fight, it would seem a questionable proceeding to try to do away with war.

In the first place, I do not think these facts prove what they are meant to prove, that fighting in itself is good for the character. If you take the world of the present day, you do not find that the societies which are always full of fighting, such as China or Mexico, are morally superior to others. Quite the reverse. You do not find in any given society that the class of man who is always fighting—say the slum rough—is morally superior to others. Again, quite the reverse. I think the truth is that, in stating the militarist case, we were drawing our evidence from semi-civilized and lawless societies in which fighting—literal fighting with sword, spear, or gun—is a necessity for self-protection, and consequently is the main test of courage, honour, discipline, and power of effort. When the Armenian gave up his arms, he did largely give up the power of defending his honour; he was left with no means of self-defence against the Turk but flattery and deceit. That was because he lived in Turkey. In a better civilization he would not have needed arms to defend himself or his honour. He would have needed the sort of character and conduct that earns the good will of civilized men. Strife or conflict is doubtless a permanent necessity in life, but as civilization advances the quality of the strife changes. If you think, among the men and women whose lives you know, of those who strike you as most remarkable for sheer courage against odds, how many of them have ever touched a weapon or needed one? They showed courage without. They "endured hardness" for the sake of what they believed to be right, and thus obtained just the same moral education that in a different society belonged to the fighting men. The test of honour also changes with civilization. A mediæval knight could apparently save his honour by killing the man who accused him of a base action; he could now only save it by proving that the accusation was false.

You may say that, nevertheless, even in modern times the instinctive thrill of admiration with which we all regard the fighting man is a proof that, in spite of the softness and artificiality with which we are surrounded, we still know in our hearts that fighting is the real test of a man, and military glory the true type of glory. But the conclusion would be quite unjustified. Romance is the oldest thing in the world. And those romantic instincts depend on habits of thought which were formed at the dawn of civilization. They are evidence, not of what is true now, but of what was true thousands of years ago.

The point that strikes one most in the behaviour of civilized man as compared with that of the savage is the immense increase of regularity and steadiness, of continuous mastery of circumstance with no falling back. It is actually true of the savage that the alternative to war or hunting is mostly idleness, with its normal accompaniments of self-indulgence and dissipation. It is the same in many Oriental societies. Tribes which have put their whole ambitions into war degenerate when compelled to live in peace. It seems to have been the same in the cruder societies of antiquity. It was a sort of new invention when the Athenians began to value "leisure" (σχολή), not as a form of idleness, but a free time in which to do one's best work—an invention which has saved civilization.

A barbaric prince will build a great tomb or palace, but neither he nor his successors will take daily care of it to see that it does not fall to bits. A civilized man will do so as a matter of course. A civilized man practises, without effort, an amount of daily self-denial, discipline, and forethought which seem to me to be more than the moral equivalent of the frequent fighting that he has lost. It is surely a very remarkable thing that civilized troops, trained in habits of peace, though probably they feel the suffering of war and hate the cruelty of war much more than the savage, nevertheless are on the whole better soldiers; that, in the late war, the immense civilian armies bore so well the utterly unaccustomed and unimagined strain to which they were subjected. Their normal life had never trained them for that: but evidently it had trained them in habits of self-respect and fortitude. Their actions proved it. I doubt if we can appreciate without a vigorous imaginative effort the degree of daily self-control and self-mastery which is necessary for a respectable lawyer or doctor or merchant or artisan in a civilized European community. To get up punctually, to do your daily work, to refrain from over-eating and over-drinking though you have superabundance of meat and drink before you, to refrain from the small dishonesties and lazinesses that offer themselves every day, to keep in your mind the probable future result of a long course of consistent and unexciting action and to behave accordingly: these things are so much a matter of course in the life of a fairly successful civilized man that we are apt to forget how difficult they are, and what a continuous discipline of character they afford. One can see the result of it in the statistics of income-tax, or the growth of schools or hospitals; one can see it in the politeness of a London crowd finding its way home in an overcrowded tube or omnibus; or, if you prefer it, on the fields of the Somme.

Judged even by the standard of war itself, the civilized man, accustomed all his life to peace, showed no deterioration. The London clerk did certainly no worse than the Sikh or Gurkha, the French *poilu* no worse than the Senegalese. Judged by almost any other standard of moral fortitude, I think he would come out better.

Consequently I do not think that there is any case to be made for the necessity of frequent fighting to modern men as a moral discipline. The moral discipline, for the majority of men who have to earn their own living, is there already. But furthermore, if such a moral discipline were really needed, I greatly doubt if modern war would give it. When Hector stood before Troy in battle, he knew all the time the purpose of his action. He faced death to save Troy from sack and Andromache from slavery. He saw the enemy in front of him, and the whole significance of his action was present to his mind: its risk, its endurance, its sacrifice of life for something dearer than life. "I care not for my life, nor for my brethren, nor Priam himself, as I care for you." But when the first enthusiasm of war is over, when a man has been wading for months in cold mud, firing at enemies he can never see, and wounded by fragments of iron coming from he knows not where, in order that of two long lists of war-aims, which he has not had the opportunity to study, one may be realized and the other not—supposing, that is, that either of them really means what it seems to say—the direct element of fighting and facing death for those whom he loves is obscured and blurred over by all kinds of other elements in his experience. No doubt in practice men fight because they are fighting, and not for a conscious cause or purpose: or just as often, they invent some mythical purpose. I remember a sergeant in 1914 who hated war but "could not let the Serbs go on murdering the Australians". To the unimaginative man the war becomes, perhaps, a matter of dull dogged endurance. To the imaginative and highly intelligent, doubtless, the cause for which he faces death may remain present; but if so, a thousand other elements of experience will be present also whose effect will be to blur and blot out the element which once made the thought of war *dulce et decorum*. One friend of mine, after long stalking and hiding behind the stones of a churchyard, successfully shot dead a mild-looking middle-aged German, and found himself merely haunted by the thought that Christ had died equally for both of them. One, taking refuge from a hail of bullets in a cellar, in which there was only just room for himself and his own platoon, had to stand at the door keeping it barred against other bodies of French and English fugitives, shutting them out into the bullet-swept street. The things that had to be done became too obviously evil. One became too like a beast of prey, only more subtle and more relentless than other beasts.

In a certain trench at Christmas men were fraternizing with the Germans; firing had stopped and the opposing parties were throwing one another small delicacies, sausages in return for pots of jam and the like; an officer coming up to stop the fraternization made a man who was about to throw a jam-pot throw a bomb instead, without warning. The man who caught it, expecting friendliness, was doubtless killed. The man who threw it was not morally ennobled; he was haunted in his dreams for years by the horror of what he had done. One pupil of mine was haunted by the remembrance of a particular night when he lay trying to sleep, but was kept awake partly by a group of soldiers—not British—sharpening their bayonets and discussing the various fantastic things they had done or would do to any wounded enemy who might fall into their hands, and partly by some little girls who walked up and down before the lines, crying "Un franc, un franc"—as a price for the violation of their childish bodies. I do not wish to dwell on horrors. I do not suppose any soldier will or can tell all the worst he knows. But one must just bear some such facts as these in mind when the claim is made that war, in present conditions, is a moral tonic.

Apart from all else, the strain is too great. A limited strain may strengthen the muscles; but a strain too hard and too long breaks them. And the strain of a war like the Great War lasting on and on, year after year, had a threefold effect. First, it broke down or overtaxed men's powers of resistance. Next, it made them forget the high motives for which at the beginning they or their elder brothers had sacrificed their comfort, their peaceful pursuits, their hopes in life; it made them accept the mere fact of living to kill Germans. Lastly, it accustomed them to the daily routine of war, with its brutalities, its narrow outlook, its wangling and humbug, its negation of conscience and liberty. It made men forget just those things which the citizen of a civilized community normally expects of his fellows and they of him.

There is one particular effect of the long war which is specially worth bearing in mind. In war, where enormous masses of men of very mixed quality are being daily compelled to do things which are constantly disagreeable and sometimes almost unbearable, they have to be set in action, if they are to act at all, by violent and immediate motives. If you do not move at once, you are sworn at and abused as no criminal is abused in civil life: if you fail in a duty, you are court-martialled: if you disobey orders or desert, you are shot; and all the time if you are not careful you are killed. Now it is one of the most distinguishing marks of a civilized and advanced community that men learn to act from gentle and remote motives. You work properly, not because you will be instantly cursed and beaten if you do not, but because on the whole, looking to the future as well as the present, working properly suits you best. You act from authoritative motives rather than violent motives: I mean, if someone makes you very angry, your wish to knock him down may be a strong motive, your reluctance to make a scene may be a weak one, but is in some sense authoritative. You feel that you ought to obey it, and you do. It seems to me, both from my own slight experience and from what I hear from others, that one of the chief reasons for the psychological dislocation and unfitness for ordinary civil employment so often produced by the war is just this inability to act except from immediate and violent motives. Accustomed, as Wordsworth puts it, to a "habit of outrageous stimulation", men grow unable to do their daily tasks without it.

The same causes, in different degrees, were operating on the civilians in England. Some of them even more strongly. We can all remember how the soldiers were sometimes afraid that the civilians would not hold out. We can remember how the soldiers were often shocked by the ferocity of the people at home. The soldiers were face to face with facts, and facts are the great educators. The soldier, if he had any passionate feeling against the enemy, had such ample means of giving vent to it. He did so much more harm, and inflicted so much more suffering, than he really wished, that his angry passions were more than satisfied. The civilian had his anger and his vicarious sufferings all bottled up, undischarged in action; consequently they boiled over in words and emotions. One must not forget, either, another great source of corruption which the Great War, like all wars, let loose. It dangled the prospect of enormous prizes before vain, ambitious or merely covetous persons. Think of the strange candidates for national eminence who were put forward by various groups or newspapers, candidates whose subsequent careers sometimes led forward to the prison or the asylum, sometimes merely back to obscurity. Think of the opportunities for corrupt gain, and the immense importance of what was called "profiteering". Think of the organized system of mendacity which developed towards the end of the war. I remember myself one small but significant incident showing the general debasement of standards. A certain educational post was created in connexion with the Army, an important post with a high salary, about which I was asked to advise. Among the candidates was one, and I think one only, who could not spell. His brief letter of application contained three mistakes, one being "Proffesor". He got the appointment.

Let me sum up so far the argument that I have put before you. In speaking of the ideal of peace, I do not understand peace as involving the absence of all strife or conflict, whether against obstacles or against human opponents. I accept fully and frankly the position that strife or conflict is a necessary element in education and the building up of character, and indeed a necessary quality of life itself. Life without strife would be mere decay. In primitive societies and in those incalculably remote ages in which human instincts were first formed, such strife took, ordinarily or obviously, the form of actual fighting, the physical battle of man against man, or man against beast, for the protection of himself or his group; and this ancient fact still naturally dominates our emotions and imaginations, and produces instinctively the supreme admiration of the soldier.

I then raise the question whether, these things being so, the continuance of war as an institution is necessary for the moral health of the human race, and whether a general renunciation of what Mr. Kipling calls "the lordliest life on earth" would result in a general flabbiness of tissue. And my answer is in the negative on three main grounds: first, that civilized life itself, under normal conditions, provides the element of strife, effort and discipline, all the more effective because it is continuous and comparatively gentle in action, instead of being sudden and violent. Second, that war under modern conditions, in which the actual cutting edge of an army is so extremely small compared with the immense mass of preparation, service and organization behind, in which aims are so complicated and the periods of warfare so prolonged, provides comparatively little of that simple and clear-cut call to sacrifice which came as a matter of course to the ancient warrior facing death for his wife and his city. And thirdly, that even if the moral stimulus were much greater than it is, it would be outweighed by the factors of moral degradation and debasement which needs must accompany modern war on a large scale and lower the whole level of civilization for years or generations afterwards.

There is really a touch of something insane in the idea that civilization or the general level of human character can best be saved and improved by war. It is like looking to famines and pestilences to secure the improvement of public health and keep the industry of doctors up to standard. It is like wishing business men to have rascally partners and bankrupt creditors, in order to secure their impeccable uprightness and fortitude in paying their debts, and thus promoting the ultimate prosperity of the country. Of course, when any great reversal of fortune occurs some good can generally be extracted from it. It may by human strength of character be made to yield some good results among its many bad. But wise education does not place its hopes in exceptional and crushing trials, which only a few superior pupils may overcome, or in rare and violent punishments which will terrify the wicked into virtue. It puts its hopes in a quiet and regular process of discipline and moral pressure, which may form gradually the habit of intelligent interest and self-mastery, and, as Plato puts it, "enjoyment of the right things". That is the sort of education our civilization ought to provide for us; not one built upon blinding disasters and the hope of heroic reactions.

But the truth is that all this semi-philosophic talk about strife has nothing, or almost nothing, to do with war in the strict sense. War is one particular development of the principle of strife, just as Bluebeard's household was one particular development of the principle of marriage.

The apologists for war—German, British, or American—get their minds badly confused because they continue to speak of war as if it were an element in human nature, like Strife or Fear or Ambition. They speak as if those who proposed to abolish war among civilized peoples were proposing to suppress the combative passions or eradicate one of the primitive instincts. The war which is formally renounced in the Pact of Paris and practically guarded against in the Covenant is not an instinct, it is a form of state action. It is not an element in human nature, it is part of a political programme. It is no more an instinct, or an element in human nature, than the adoption of an income-tax, or state-owned railways, or a protective tariff on wheat. And further, it is a form of state action which may at one time have been profitable to one of the parties engaged, but under modern conditions is indubitably disastrous to both. Even supposing that it still was the best of all moral tonics, the plain fact would remain that, however desirable, war is a luxury which modern civilization cannot afford. War may once have acted as a safety-valve, letting off superfluous energy. It is now an explosion wrecking the whole machine. This fact is generally admitted, but the causes of it are perhaps not always understood.[1]

The fundamental condemnation of war, I venture to think, is not its expense, not its waste of life, not even its dysgenic influence on the race in destroying the fit and preserving the unfit: it is that it is incompatible with civilization. War interrupts and makes impossible the main task of mankind, the twofold task of raising the level of individual character and power so as to make possible the formation of a better society; and of organizing society in better ways, so as to call forth higher qualities in the individuals who are its citizens. This is very cold and general language. I can make it more definite if I speak of various pupils of mine, men of quite first-rate character and intellect who went to the war and were killed, for the most part as Second-Lieutenants. They were debarred by the war from giving their best gifts to the world; England became for the time a society to which such gifts were of no use. One

[1] See below, Lecture VII, pp. 222 ff.

was a philosopher and a born teacher; I do not know in which direction he would have developed most. One was a tutor to the Workers' Educational Association: he had refused positions with much higher salaries and prospects because he saw in this educational ferment of the working classes the greatest enterprise for his own powers and the greatest hope for England. One was chiefly devoted (like myself) to interpreting and keeping alive the beauty of a great literature that might otherwise be forgotten. One would have been a great and humane lawyer. Two or three were in the Civil Service, at home or abroad, helping to administer and build up that magnificent, though imperfect, Commonwealth under which we live. Others were writers. One was a musician. Some were in business of various sorts. All were in their different ways helping in that main task of mankind. For of course it is a shallow view which thinks of a good merchant or banker or trader as merely engaged in "making money", and fails to see that he is maintaining, by means of systematic competence and honesty, a vast system of credit and mutual trust throughout the world without which civilization would come to wreck. "Don't think", Dr. Jowett used to warn young enthusiasts, "don't think that life consists in doing good; it doesn't." He meant that the main work of life lies in carrying on worthily the great common task of civilization: to play one's due part in the enterprise of feeding some hundreds of millions of men, in seeing that they are protected against violence and fraud, that they have access to justice, and as far as may be to education, that they have some freedom to pursue life and happiness, and are not cut off altogether from the wonders and beauties of the world and the mind of man. To succeed in doing this is civilization: to fail is the defeat of civilization. For civilization is, ultimately, the process whereby a human society in search, as Aristotle puts it, of a "good life for man", gradually overcomes the obstacles, material and other, that stand in its way and makes man increasingly master of his environment. The strife to attain this end is the strife to which I would look for the moral equivalent of war in the formation and strengthening of character. True, it may be, except to the adventurer, or poet or artist, a struggle with comparatively few ecstatic moments, few of those "crowded hours of glorious life" on which the poet puts such a high and perhaps excessive value; but it is one in which every step counts, every weakness or cowardice has its result, and in which surely the greater advances are never won nor the greater disasters averted without the facing of much risk and the acceptance of much personal sacrifice.

Of course, we must not exaggerate. It is easy enough for the poet or artist to realize the eternal value of that beauty which he loves and, if he is fortunate, creates or interprets. But no doubt it is true that an ordinary man in his daily round does not keep thinking, he mostly does not even realize, that he is playing the part of some tiny wheel or screw in the works of this enormous engine; that by catching his train and paying his bills and doing his best to live a clean, honest, and sober life, he is contributing to the stability of the British Empire and even to that of human civilization. It needs an effort of imagination or of philosophy to see things in that way. But a very large number of men are more or less vividly conscious of that part of the machine in which they are immediately engaged—the credit of the firm, the prestige of the regiment, the good name of the family—and do more or less identify its future with their own. The motive works, in one form or another. And apart from occasional conflicts between different parts, it is a motive steadily working for good.

This service of civilization is our true work; the occupation that gives meaning to life. We need peace, inward and outward, because peace leaves us free to attend to it; while war—or, indeed, any violent hatred—interrupts and wrecks and perverts. The secret of life, it may well be conjectured, lies in the finding of some end to work for which is at least relatively permanent and unaffected by the brevity and transience of our own physical powers. To have lived so that something which we love and serve may live after us, that great ideal act of sacrifice which makes the soldier the hero of our imaginative literature, can be realized also in the service of civilization, wherever that service is faithful to the end.

Is it pedantic, is it the mere result of my special education, that I fall back again upon Aristotle? He tells us that Happiness in the highest sense, or the true end of human life, is first activity, next unimpeded activity, and lastly unimpeded activity "according to virtue"; that is to say, on right lines and for good ends. Surely we want, both as individuals and as a community, to pursue that quest for the attainment or the creation of "a good life for man"; we want to get to that work unhindered and uncrippled, and therefore, apart from other reasons, we need above all things peace.

II

THE CIVILIZATION OF THE NINETEENTH CENTURY: ITS GREATNESS AND THE FLAW WHICH LED TO ITS COLLAPSE

As we get farther away from the England of the nineteenth century, and see it separated from us by the great gulf of the war, we shall perhaps be better able to see it as it really was, to appreciate its extraordinary greatness, its peculiar faults and flaws, and to a remarkable degree its unity.

Beyond question it was a very great age indeed. For Great Britain especially it marked the zenith of national success, the widest expansion over the world of British government, British commerce, British political thought, British morals, philosophy, science, poetry and prose literature. It was a time when Indian rajahs and Chinese mandarins learnt to play cricket and read Macaulay, as now they are learning baseball and frequenting the movies. The material advance in population, wealth, shipping, commerce, etc., is simply overwhelming, and needs no illustration. The advance in scientific discovery, first in mechanics and physics, later in biology, is probably without a parallel in the history of the world. The advance in humanity and care for the alleviation of suffering is also, so far as I know, without a parallel: in England alone in this period we find the abolition of slavery—at the cost of £20,000,000 of public money willingly given; the sweeping reform of the old criminal law and the barbarous penal system which accompanied it. In 1818 about 1 in every 200 of the population was in prison; a hundred years later, with a far more efficient police, it was about 1 in 2,000. We find the reform in the treatment of lunatics; the laws against cruelty to children and to animals; the Factory Acts; the Married Women's Property Acts; the immense spread of education in all its stages, both by public authority and by private experiment; the beginnings of the care for public health; the greatly increased consumption of coffee, tea, fruit, and light viands, along with a greatly decreased consumption of alcohol. An interesting study might be made of the effects on society of the discovery of safe anæsthetics. The use of anæsthetics has doubtless made men in general more sensitive to pain in themselves and others; but one must also realize that the determination of doctors to find and to use some safe anæsthetic was more directly the result of an increasing reluctance to inflict pain on their patients than of any inability to bear it themselves when they happened to be patients. The discovery was quite as much due to the increase of humanity as a cause of that increase afterwards. In poetry the nineteenth century from Wordsworth and Shelley to Tennyson, Browning and Swinburne, must, I think, fairly be recognized as either the greatest or the second greatest age in the history of English literature; in prose it was indisputably the time in which the English novel, from Scott and Jane Austen to Dickens, Thackeray and Meredith, burst into bloom at home and sallied forth successfully to conquer Europe. In painting, opinions will be divided: much may be said from the strictly technical side against the great Victorian painters, but it probably remains true that such artists as Watts and Millais and Burne-Jones did somehow interpret in a very rare degree the higher imagination of their time.

What reason, then, what strange reason, is it that fills the pages of our minor contemporary writers with an open contempt for the Victorian Era or the whole nineteenth century? It is worth discussing, though I doubt if I can find any complete answer. One contributing cause may be the wish of rebels to find some name for the thing they want to rebel against; and the word "Victorian", with its suggestion of a repressive and somewhat reactionary lady in her declining years, has for the purpose many advantages. There are certain obvious political prejudices: for it was, of course, the great age of Liberalism. There is also the natural opposition felt at the time of any change of fashion between the old and the new. It is perhaps difficult for people who are not acutely conscious of their own clothes or furniture to understand the strength of feeling with which a young man, full of excitement over his wide pink flannel trousers, may regard those who have not taken the same plunge, or with which young householders, flushed with pride over a drawing-room with black walls and one picture, may look upon a Morris pomegranate paper and a crowd of watercolours. But these are trivialities.

A more serious cause can be seen in the reaction against Victorian earnestness. In Bernard Shaw's *Quintessence of Ibsenism* it is remarked that there are two kinds of moral reformers. One discovers that something which most people do is wrong and must not be done. He, says Mr. Shaw, is publicly praised and secretly hated. The other proclaims that something hitherto condemned and forbidden is really harmless, and there is no reason why you should not do it if you like. This man is publicly condemned and reprobated; in secret he is adored by all the people whom he has, so to speak, set free. Now the Victorian Age, or the nineteenth century as a whole, was a great moral reformer of the first type. It proclaimed that men, even courtiers and noblemen, ought not to be drunken or dissolute or even corrupt, that politics were really concerned with the welfare of the people, and that the rich had duties towards the poor. The transition from George IV and his unpleasing brothers to the young Queen and the Prince Consort was typical of a much wider change. When Lord Palmerston was caught chasing a maid of honour into her bedroom, the excuse made for him was: "Your Majesty should remember that he is a very old gentleman and accustomed to the manners of the late Court". And it would be a complete mistake to suppose that the change was a mere increase in decorum.

There was a re-birth of public spirit. Gentlemen ceased to take bribes. Justice became incorruptible. Literature not only observed a reticence in language and subject which had already begun in the late eighteenth century, but was inspired by the spirit that we rather vaguely term "idealism". It has been observed that up to about 1820 the laws passed by Parliament had almost all been for the protection of the privileged few against the many; after that time they are predominantly for the protection of the nation as a whole against abuse and privilege. Instead of the ferocious defence of property, a spirit of sympathy and help to the oppressed begins to inspire legislation. The old revolutionary doctrine of the infinite perfectibility of mankind, which had set on fire the enthusiasm of Godwin, Shelley and Condorcet, passed in a milder and more reasonable form into the general imagination of the age. Whether or no man might be made perfect, he certainly might be made better and happier than he is; and the conscious pursuit of that object became an accepted source of inspiration to politics and literature. With it went the conception that the necessary condition of the pursuit was freedom: set man free, let him have room to move and external conditions which do not starve or cramp him, and human nature of itself will strive to rise higher. This spirit shows itself in almost all the best English fiction of the period, from romantics, like the Brontës, and realists, like George Eliot, to satirists, like Dickens and Thackeray. It had been utterly lacking in Fielding and Smollett, and even in Jane Austen. It shows itself in the immense increase of charitable institutions, of religious missions, of societies for the education of the people. There is no question of hypocrisy. To suppose there is, is the mere petulance of jealousy. Shelley's or Gladstone's love of moral improvement was just as genuine as Falstaff's love of sack. But an age of moral earnestness seems in our own day to have been succeeded by an age of relaxation; and one can see in, for instance, such a book as Mr. Strachey's *Eminent Victorians* that the moral earnestness of Gladstone or Dr. Arnold is felt by the author to be a hateful quality and not easily forgiven. One seems to see the resentment of an over-tired man against a muscular and energetic walking companion.

That, I think, is an element to be borne in mind and liberally discounted, because, after all, it is the resentment of the inferior against the superior for being superior. But none the less there is in the criticism that is now launched against the Victorian Age one element which is perfectly sound and valid, though it detracts but little from the real greatness of that time. In almost every department of human activity we feel that the nineteenth century, for all its magnificent achievement, does not quite satisfy us. After all, how could it, unless we were all dead or asleep? We have gone on practising the same arts, studying the same problems; and of course we have in most cases discovered some new facts or thought out some new piece of technique. Thousands of people have been working at Darwin's subject, and naturally they have found some things to correct in him, though none of them may be as great a discoverer as Darwin. A modern novelist can show many tiresome tricks of style, superficialities of observation, or defects of analysis in Dickens or Thackeray, Meredith or Hardy, but would not therefore pretend to be able to write better novels. Every honours student of philosophy at any British university has learnt to summarize the inconsistencies of John Stuart Mill; most art students can point out the improvements in technique made by Sargent as compared with Turner or Millais, though he may be less convincing when he expounds the further immense improvement made on Sargent by some more recent idol. I am not clear that any recent poet can claim to surpass Tennyson, or even Browning, in sheer mastery of technique, but he can at any rate demand some change of subjects or some less old-fashioned ideas. This is all true. To some extent one may say it is really a matter of course. In every society that has any life in it, each succeeding age must be able to show some points of advance upon the last. The age of Dryden was in literary power far inferior to that of Shakespeare, but it could point out convincingly the faults of Elizabethan prose and poetry. None the less, when all these allowances are made, I think that in the Victorian Age, or the nineteenth century as a whole, there is one real weakness on which later criticism has seized quite justly and correctly. It is the defect that belongs naturally to its great virtue. It was so creative that it forgot to criticize. It was so sanguine that it overlooked flaws and dangers; so confident in its achievements that it preferred to acquiesce in a comfortable faith rather than vex its spirit with the search for a strictly consistent philosophy.

The sort of optimist view of the world which runs through most of the great Victorian writers and statesmen seems to me to be based on the ideal dreams of the Revolution modified, not by any philosophical analysis, but by an instinct of moderation and common sense. Godwin and Condorcet had real philosophies, which ended either in smoke or in disasters. Macaulay and Sidney Smith had in their hearts much the same philosophy; but they never believed in it enough to do anything really foolish. They did on the whole think it likely that if you were virtuous you would be happy; that education would remove most moral evils; that the voice of the people was likely to be right; that an increase of freedom would bring about probably an increase of virtue and almost certainly an improvement in government. But they did not trust theory when it conflicted with experience, and they would always sooner be inconsistent than obviously wrong. "I have a passionate love", said Sidney Smith, "for common justice and common sense." You cannot make a philosophy out of that, but you can make a most excellent rule of conduct. Macaulay and Hallam conceived of English history as a logical development of constitutional freedom up to the principles of the Revolution of 1689; such a view is philosophically almost grotesque, since the Revolution of 1689 was a complicated compromise dependent on very peculiar circumstances. It was not the expression of an eternal principle. Yet for practical purposes it was probably the best conception of English history that had yet been struck out, the wisest, the most practical, the most full of hope for the future. Hegel had given a far more profound interpretation of human history, but it has never been of use, as far as I know, to anyone. Nietzsche had given one far more consistent and subtle, but it was mad. The English nineteenth-century view of the world was apt to be shallow, apt to be inconsistent, but it worked. It was true to "common justice" and "common sense". It seldom or never did harm; in almost all great crises it was—to use a golfing metaphor—"as good as a better".

Let us take one signal instance: the religious teaching established in state schools by the Act of 1870. There were two or three possible views which might claim to be logical. If Parliament knew what religious doctrine was true, it should have that doctrine taught in the schools; presumably it would be that of the Church of England. If Parliament did not know what religion was true, it could either abstain from religious teaching altogether and have lay schools, as in France, or it could allow all sects to have a right of entry to the schools in order to inculcate their particular preferences. Parliament did none of these things. It accepted a motion from a private member, Mr. Cowper Temple, authorizing the teaching of Christianity, but ordaining that "no religious catechism or religious formulary distinctive of any particular denomination shall be taught in the schools". Disraeli, out for mischief as usual, riddled the clause with hostile criticism. It was unintelligible; it founded, on the spur of the moment, a new religion; it made the teachers into a new sacerdotal class. Yet as a matter of fact the clause expressed the real fundamental wish of the best minds of the nineteenth century, it stood the test of experience, it enabled religious teaching to move as men's aspirations moved, and it did in a rough-and-ready way separate the kernel of religion from the husk of dogmatic theology. Established religions do not cut a very distinguished figure in the history of human thought, but that unconsciously created by Mr. Cowper Temple is perhaps, for practical purposes, about the best there has ever been.

Do not suppose that I am praising the lack of logic in itself, or that the statesmen and others whom I am praising actually prided themselves on lack of logic. Quite the contrary. They tried hard to be as logical as they could. Every reasonably intelligent person does. The difference between what is called the "practical Anglo-Saxon mind" and the "logical Latin mind" is that the Latin sometimes tends to take one single line of thought and follow it to its logical result, whereas the Englishman, at his best, takes into consideration a great many lines of thought, covering as far as possible all the relevant facts, and, since some point one way and some another, does not attempt to follow any one of them to the bitter end. He tries to give due weight to all factors, and to act in such a way that one mistake will not be fatal. But he is not absolved from the duty of thinking as closely and logically as he can about each element of the problem.

This was, I would suggest, what the Victorian Age characteristically did. It cared more for life than for thought; consequently it produced abundant and fine life, while its thought was comparatively unambitious and aimed mainly at serving the practical purposes of life. It cared intensely for morals and little for metaphysics; a good deal for religion and scarcely at all for theology; and since morals depend ultimately on metaphysics and religion on theology, it left always a large extent of vague and misty margin in the beliefs which it held most firmly. It had an immense faith, a faith in goodness, in duty, in the future of mankind. It believed with a certain passion in the maxims of the copybook or even the nursery, and where these led to awkward or puzzling consequences it took refuge in a masterly reticence. It realized especially the immense value of reticence in art. In its imaginative literature it almost ignored dirt, it ignored obscenity, it ignored all the multitudinous vibrations of meanness, spite, and sensuality below the threshold which so enchain and almost monopolize the attention of many modern writers. And, since its creative power was gigantic, it created a world of imaginative literature in which these things were practically non-existent. Or perhaps I am wrong in saying that the nineteenth-century artists ignored these things: they knew them, probably, well enough; but at least they were reticent about them. Shelley knew all about the suppressed horrors under the threshold of consciousness;[1] Dickens and Thackeray knew well the seamy sides of life. They could even produce, for artistic purposes, the full effect of it with extreme economy of means. In the midst of so much habitual reticence every word told.

In politics there was the same reticence, the same idealism. Where a social evil could be dealt with they talked about it; otherwise not. It is curious how little Peel or Gladstone or Lord Salisbury, from their public utterances, would seem ever to have realized the deeper horrors and cruelties of the *res publica*. A friend of mine who proposed standing as a Labour candidate in 1918 was, after a speech full of eloquence and sympathy, told to stand down: the audience did not want "any of that damned middle-class idealism". It was the Victorian Age condemned by that which came after: the "middle-class idealism" of people who did not suffer, but sympathized with suffering and wished to be good, condemned by people who

[1] See *Prometheus*, Act I, 483-491, and the whole scene.

themselves suffered and hated those who did not suffer, and did not in the least care to be good. One can see the same uncritical idealism in the painting of the Victorians. It is literary, emotional, imaginative, at times even intentionally edifying. Thousands of people loved Watts's *Hope* or Burne-Jones's *Merciful Knight*, but more for their poetry than for their painting. Science itself was humane and sanguine. So strong was the spirit of the age, that science swallowed its great new discovery of the struggle for life and the survival of the fittest with hardly a shudder, hardly a moment's interruption in its vision of universal benevolence. The struggle merely led to "scientific meliorism", with George Eliot as its imaginative prophet. Business was optimistic, adventurous, full of self-congratulation—much as it is now in America. A later time found it full of weaknesses, ignorant of foreign languages and foreign customs, unwilling to take intellectual trouble or even to believe that intellect in any form was much good; but in its day, by its very faith and confidence and cheerful enterprise, it attained a degree of prosperity never before known in the world.

Now the point I wish to bring out is this: One finds in the history of human civilization a constant alternation between two processes—first organization and then disorganization; in the language of biology, first anabolism and then katabolism; first the slow building up of an ordered social structure or cosmos, then the reduction of that cosmos into chaos. No human cosmos endures very long. If it is not shattered by invasion or civil war or external disaster, it is undermined by the advance of knowledge, by the growth of social elements hitherto neglected and making for confusion, by some inherent contradiction in its own basis, or the like. The Chinese philosophers, I find, have a conception that is similar, though not quite the same. They say that a period of *Yin*, the female principle, peaceful, continuous, anabolic, is regularly followed by one of *Yang*, the male principle, violent, shattering and katabolic, but creative. *Yin* is very pleasant, but if it lasts too long it means stagnation and decay.

The conception is not an unfamiliar one. The Greek City State was a cosmos; it produced a world in which the good citizen knew exactly how to behave; it was overthrown by a chaos of military conquests, in which no one felt clear what to think or what to do. The Roman Empire was a cosmos; its break-up a chaos. The mediæval conception of the unity of Christendom under the Pope and the Emperor was, in conception, a cosmos, though one that failed before it was realized. In our own day, travellers often tell us of a Polynesian or African tribe, living in good order, with a fixed social system and a code of conduct which is duly respected: that is cosmos. Then they tell how the same tribe is plunged into dissolution by the advent of the White Man. It is not merely the introduction of drink and Western vices that does the destruction; it is the bewildering contact with a stronger and more complex civilization. To take a very simple example, a certain tribe of Eskimo in Alaska lived till lately a peaceful, orderly and contented life, hunting the seal and dependent on it for almost everything. The seal gave them their food, their light, their fuel, their clothes, their houses, and many of their tools. Then American traders came to them. They did nothing obviously bad. They did not plunder them or teach them to drink; they merely offered a good price for sealskins. The Eskimo proceeded to kill more seals in order to sell the skins; they bought guns in order to kill them faster; they have by now nearly exterminated the animal on which they depend and are living in a state of extreme misery and distraction. Cosmos has, by the introduction of one new factor, been reduced to chaos.

Now I wish to suggest that the Victorian Era was in the main a cosmos, an ordered unity, and that we have witnessed its breakdown. In a later chapter I will develop the idea further. I do not, of course, suggest that the cosmos was complete. There were all sorts of flaws and excrescences in it. For one thing, as Mr. and Mrs. Hammond have shown in a striking book, the Industrial Revolution, which began at the end of the eighteenth century, was itself a dissolvent force, breaking up the order of country life, with its mutual ties and duties, as it had existed for many generations, and substituting a life of mere economic struggle.

That is true; and the nineteenth century, though it grappled hard with the chaos of the industrial revolution, never quite conquered or assimilated it. No political or social cosmos is ever complete. If it were, I presume we should have that condition of stable equilibrium which is fatal to further progress, and "one good custom would corrupt the world". There were obviously great social inequalities in the Victorian Age, but the general will was steadily working to remove them. The power of wealth was too great, but was being steadily reduced. The state of public education and intelligence was rather low, but was constantly and vigorously rising. The representation of the people, on which so much depended, was still imperfect. The system of parliamentary government was, though much the best system yet invented for governing a state, in its essence far from ideal. (I sometimes think of it as rather like a parody of trial by jury, with no rules of evidence, no judge to guide the contest, any number of self-appointed advocates, and a jury wandering in and out of court at will, mostly attending to other things but listening to the evidence when it sounds spicy.) The actual rapidity of progress during most of the century makes it more difficult to speak of a fixed order, and if we speak of a spirit instead of an order, as constituting the cosmos, we must remember that it was a spirit of great freedom, admitting and encouraging the expression of most diverse opinions.

THE NINETEENTH CENTURY 57

But it was not for any of these reasons that the Victorian Cosmos actually failed. True, the vices of the industrial revolution were not worked out of its blood, and might in the course of time have proved fatal. Other causes, such as the advance of knowledge, and the industrialization of the East, were at work, and we are feeling their effects now. But none of these imperfections was the cause of the Great War. The Great War was due to another flaw in the political and social organization of Europe, a flaw perfectly definite and easily distinguishable: the belief in the independent sovereign state. It was a comparatively new belief.

There was a time (wrote Mr. Lowes Dickinson in 1917) when the whole civilized world of the West lay at peace under a single ruler, when the idea of separate sovereign states, always at war or in armed peace, would have seemed as monstrous and absurd as it now seems inevitable. And that great achievement of the Roman Empire left, when it sank, a sunset glow over the turmoil of the Middle Ages. Never would a mediæval churchman or statesman have admitted that the independence of states was an ideal. It was an obstinate tendency struggling into existence against all the preconceptions and beliefs of the time. "One Church, one Empire" was the ideal of Charlemagne, of Otho, of Barbarossa, of Hildebrand, of Thomas Aquinas, of Dante. The forces struggling against that ideal were the enemy to be defeated. They won. And thought, always parasitic on action, endorsed the victory. So that there is now hardly a philosopher or historian who does not urge that the sovereignty of independent states is the last word of political fact and political wisdom. No doubt in some respects (he continues) there has been an advance. In so far as there are real nations, and these are coincident with states, it is well that they should develop freely their specific gifts and characters. The good future of the world is not with uniformity, but with diversity. But it should be well understood that all the diversity required is compatible with political union. The idea of the future is Federation, and to that ideal all the significant facts of the present point.

These seem to me wise words. But for the moment I wish merely to emphasize the main salient defect of the system of independent sovereign states. I will not consider its effect on the ordinary course of daily business; the incessant interruption to trade and intercourse and the course of justice caused by tariffs, passport regulations, national prejudices and the lack of any common legal system or international police. I will not try to explain the quaint fact that there are in most countries Ministers of State appointed for no purpose whatever but to make these interruptions worse. I will not dwell on the immense expense to each nation and the nervous friction in international relations caused by the fact that every sovereign state has, or had in the nineteenth century, a perfect right to declare war on another for any cause and at any moment, so that consequently they had all to be always ready for defence. I will only take the one point in the system which I think did actually prove fatal to the cosmos of the nineteenth century.

Suppose that inside a state there is a dispute between individuals. The parties are not allowed to fight. They generally have common friends or acquaintances who are anxious to pacify both sides, to explain to each the other's point of view, and thus to settle the matter out of court. At the worst, if they cannot be induced to agree, they go to law. The case for each is carefully expounded to the tribunal; the witnesses are heard, the statements tested and sifted; and eventually a decision is given by a competent and impartial third person.

Suppose a conflict of classes: this takes us into the political arena. There will be debates in Parliament, where each side will have the opportunity, and probably repeated opportunities, of stating its case. They will state it again on the platform at political meetings. It will be discussed repeatedly in the Press. In the end the matter will be decided by a Parliament elected by a free vote from both parties. I do not say that the conditions will be exactly equal. In any conflict between what are called "workers" and "capitalists" the capitalists will have most of the newspapers and the workers by far the most of the voters. But speaking generally, when a conflict occurs inside a state, a machinery will be set immediately to work, and will work continuously, to secure that both sides of the dispute shall be properly stated and the ultimate decision made by representatives of the whole nation to which both the disputants belong. The system works for fair discussion, full inquiry, and an impartial decision.

On the other hand, suppose there is a conflict of interests between two sovereign independent states; in that case the political machinery works all wrong. Imagine a dispute, under pre-war conditions, between France and England. The French newspapers, getting their information from French sources, state the French point of view in such a way as to please patriotic Frenchmen. The English newspapers, getting their information from English sources, do the opposite; and all patriotic Englishmen, already, of course, inclined to back their own country, are supplied daily with arguments to support their prejudice and incitements to make it keener. Meantime the statesmen on both sides are at work. It may well be that they would like to be reasonable, but, under the present democratic system, the existence of every Government depends on its popularity with the people of its own country. The opinion of foreigners does not count. So the English statesmen, under penalty of losing popularity, must state and restate the English side of the case so as to please Englishmen, and Englishmen already semi-intoxicated by the reading of English newspapers and no others. On the other side of the Channel it is just the same. The French statesmen, if they want to remain in public life, must show themselves passionately in favour of France and bravely defiant towards their overbearing and perjured neighbours. If a public man on either side states the issue impartially and critically, he suffers in popularity: if he states his country's case with obvious passion and prejudice, he does not suffer. He may be impulsive, but his heart is in the right place. It will do him no harm with his own people if those of the other nation call him a liar, and not much if they prove the statement. The proof will not be attended to. Thus the dispute itself is carried on in the worst possible way, all the machinery working so as to make both parties more unreasonable.

At last comes the decision: and the decision is made, not by any impartial or common body, but by each of the disputants separately, in a national parliament whose main anxiety is to make sure that their own nation shall have the best of it. It seems at first sight impossible for any dispute, treated on such lines, to end in anything but war. The wonder is, not that the nineteenth-century system eventually broke down, but that it managed to survive so many years and to overcome so many international difficulties. Systems are, after all, run by men; and men have both consciences and reasoning power.

It may seem as if I had exaggerated the purely nationalist influences at work in the leading countries; but I doubt if this is so. I can hardly remember a single case in which any British Minister or public character has intervened in an international controversy for the purpose of explaining the point of view of the other nation without incurring some degree of condemnation and unpopularity. I remember a case in which there was acute danger of war with a certain Great Power, and two important Ministers, to their credit, held out for peace against the majority of the Cabinet; having gained his point and made peace safe, one of these Ministers went to the country and made a passionate and inflammatory speech in order to appease public opinion and let it down easily! Everybody will have noticed that international settlements always become more difficult on the eve of a General Election or any similar crisis. The Government is then appealing to the nation as judge: and, like any other individual or group, the nation, when judging in its own cause, debarred from hearing the other side, and surrounded by advocates working and speaking in its own interest and expecting rewards for doing so, is an extremely one-sided and prejudiced judge.

It is not, of course, a new idea; but it is at any rate an idea which in modern Europe has been confined till lately to a very limited circle of thinking people, that any nation should seriously try to be just to other nations. The man who does so must be prepared for trouble. I read lately in one of the very best English literary journals a review of a book on the League of Nations, in which the author explained that he tried to take a strictly international point of view; the reviewer severely remarked that such a point of view was unworthy of an Englishman and would never suit the British reader.

I do not think the badness of the system can be seriously exaggerated. It is not merely that in every dispute between sovereign independent states each state is absolute judge in its own cause; beyond that, each is stimulated artificially by enormous and unceasing propaganda to be sure to do itself full justice. If it has not led more consistently and unvaryingly to disaster, one must remember that bad tendencies are constantly checked by good tendencies and bad systems saved by the good people who work them. It is to the interest of doctors that we should all be ill; but doctors do not, as a matter of fact, often try to make us all ill. It is to the interest of undertakers that many more of us should die, but undertakers do not, as a matter of fact, conspire together to increase the death-rate. Statesmen, and even newspaper proprietors, are human and have some conscience. Then again there are the regular diplomats and members of the Foreign Offices whose professional pride is generally involved in getting difficulties settled, who mostly know the diplomats of other countries and appreciate their points of view, who face problems seriously as business realities and not as opportunities for patriotic rhetoric or the turning out of Governments. There is an instructive story in Viscount Grey's *Twenty-Five Years* about the Ambassadors' Conference at the end of the Balkan wars in 1912–13. The question arose whether a certain frontier village named Djakova should belong to Albania or Serbia. Few people had ever heard of Djakova; none could pretend that it was important. But the Russian Press and Government had said it was Serbian, the Austrian Press and Government had said it was Albanian.

Each side was committed; patriotic feeling had grown hot; peace was endangered and settlement impossible until either the Russian representative or the Austrian could receive instructions to give way. At the end of much tension, Count Mensdorff came one morning to Sir Edward Grey: "He entered briskly, even a little breathless with haste, delighted with the good news he brought," and exclaiming that it was all right. "We give up Djakova." I have no doubt that if the Russian Government had given it up the Russian Ambassador would also have been equally delighted. What the sensible diplomat wanted was to settle the business sensibly: it was the Government, the national Press and the national opinion—all the direct expressions of the independent sovereign state—that insisted on playing for prestige. Of course, it may sometimes happen that a particular diplomat may have private ambitions or sinister designs; if so, he is very dangerous. But in general I regard the professionals, independent of public opinion and judged only by their colleagues and superiors, as a pretty sound influence. Much the same with traders and financiers. It may occur— as it did in the Boer War—that particular groups of financiers and speculative traders make the mistake of thinking that a war will pay them and deliberately helping to bring it about: but normally war is ruinous for commerce and desperately dangerous to international finance. The average influence of trade and finance must certainly be a stabilizing influence, not a wrecking one. And in public opinion itself, ill-informed as it is and apt to be perverted by national interests and prejudices, there is an element not only of conscience but—what is more important—of scepticism and common sense.

Yet in spite of all these influences the war came. In spite of the fact that a strongly pacific Government was in power in England, full of Ministers who were habitually denounced in the popular Press as "pacifists" and "friends of every country but their own"; in spite of the recent election in France, which had cut down military expenditure and reduced the period of military service from three years to two; in spite of the great and increasing strength of the Socialist Party in Germany, deeply pledged to international peace in congress after congress; in spite of the long habits of peace in Belgium, so deeply ingrained that, I am told by one who was present, the troops could not at first bring themselves to obey the order to fire on the massed Germans; in spite of the well-known love of peace in the old Austrian Emperor and the almost fanatical devotion of the Czar to the idea of peace and international arbitration; in spite of the immense growth of the peace feeling in all civilized nations and the utter strangeness, repulsiveness, and remoteness from life of the very notion of war, the fatal system acted and the war came. I do not for a moment mean that all persons concerned were equally guilty: such a view implies a complete abandonment of the duty of thinking and weighing evidence. It is plain, for instance, that the British Government worked hard and resourcefully to maintain the peace, and that militarist influences were much stronger in some countries than others. But in the main the war occurred, not because certain individuals were wicked, but because the international system was wrong.

Out of that disaster arose inevitably the demand that, when once the war was over, the system should be changed. The form of that change, a form dictated by the practical necessities of the problem, will be the subject of the next chapter.

III

THE FELT NEED. THE THREE PRINCIPLES OF THE COVENANT: CONFERENCE, LAW, SANCTIONS

THE international system of the nineteenth century had proved itself to be unworthy, both intellectually and morally, of the men and women who lived under it. It had landed the world in disaster: consequently there arose a general demand that the system should be changed.

The demand was at first confused and took some little time to clarify itself. People began, as they usually do, by repeating something which they were in the habit of saying, however irrelevant it might be. One gifted writer proposed that all Parliaments and Foreign Offices should be abolished and international problems decided by a special conference composed principally of working men, especially agricultural labourers, who had no knowledge and consequently could have no prejudices. A fairly strong movement pressed the view that all the trouble came from political institutions being not sufficiently democratic: a theory superficially plausible but fundamentally irrelevant. Democracy deals effectively with domestic disputes because it secures that in any difference between classes both parties shall be represented. It is useless in international disputes. If Greece is in conflict with Bulgaria, no amount of democracy will secure the representation of Greece in the Bulgarian Parliament or of Bulgaria in the Greek. Nor is it true, as a matter of fact, that democratic statesmen can be relied on to show an international spirit: Gambetta and Hyndman were violently nationalist, Wellington and Castlereagh were peacemakers. The counter movement to this from the other side was partly a claim that Liberal or pacific Governments always got nations into war; only a firm aggressive militarism would prevent it. In part it was a semi-articulate rejoicing, noticeable alike in England and Germany and not without repercussions in France, that, war having at last come, the ruling classes must really rule and put down this democratic tomfoolery. Such movements are chiefly of interest because of their historical consequences after the war. The one gave impetus to revolution, the other to Fascism.

Among the proposals which, whether entirely wise or not, were at least relevant to the evil they were intended to cure, we may notice three:

One was the simple and straightforward prohibition of war, with no further provisions. This view was well stated on the ground of historical precedent by Professor A. F. Pollard:—

> The analogy comes from the somewhat distant past when men were striving to find some alternative to private war as a means of settling claims to property, just as we are to-day seeking another means than war of settling international disputes. I refer to the social circumstances amid which Henry II succeeded to the throne. The civil war of Stephen's reign had produced as many

claimants, on an average, to each estate as there now are to Constantinople, to Fiume, or to Lemburg; and then, as now, the arbitrament recognized by custom was the sword for gentlemen of honour or the ordeal for less military folk. The claimant challenged the possessor to single combat, and the defendant had to fight or forfeit his title; he was never secure except in his preparedness for battle, and, to quote Bernhardi's statement of modern militarist doctrine, "what was right was determined by the arbitrament of war". How and in what order of procedure did Henry II deal with the problem? . . . There was no standing army at the Crown's disposal for the purpose, no police, no public opinion; and the combatants were as much addicted and inured to the arbitrament of the sword as nations are to-day.

He did not attempt to create a new constitution, but limited himself to practical matters of detail. He provided possessors of land with a new writ out of Chancery, called the writ *de pace habenda*. This, without any inquiry into the merits of the case, placed at their disposal whatever resources the Crown might possess as a protection against a challenge; it simply prohibited aggression. . . . Its value lay in its natural consequences. There were claimants with a good title just as there were possessors with a bad; and they naturally came to Henry with the justice of their case. . . . And he provided a further method of procedure, this time for the claimant. It was to the effect that he might have a writ ordering the election of jurors, sworn to declare the facts as they knew them, and requiring both the parties to abide by their decision.

The consequences were incalculable. Applied at first merely to cases of property and possession in land, the method of trial by jury was gradually extended to almost every department of judicature; and the habit of argument slowly superseded the custom of fighting.[1]

This interesting idea was revived some ten years later in the form of the Kellogg Pact. It was not accepted at the time because of an essential

[1] *The League of Nations: An Historical Argument*, 1918, pp. 52 ff.

difference between the domestic and the international problem. In England, when a baron broke the law and made war on his neighbour, even if the military power of the King was not sufficient to turn the scale of victory, the King's authority was there, and the King's judges were at hand to inquire into the case and correct injustice. The private war could, as a matter of fact, be crushed, and the domestic wrong righted. But in the case of a grave international conflict there was in the first place no international authority with any force at its disposal at all, and in the second place no international tribunal to inquire and pronounce judgment, according to law, much less an international legislature to make a new law where one was wanted. It seemed clear that war could not be prevented by a mere prohibition, if the seeds of war were allowed to continue. The absolute prohibition of private war remains, I think, an essential factor in any settlement. The very essence of international order is that no state shall take into its own hands the righting by force of its alleged grievances. We need an international writ *de pace habenda*. But the prohibition was not likely to work as a remedy until new and better remedies were made possible.

The prohibition of war leads almost inevitably to the proposals for the prevention of war by force. This idea of the armed coercion of the law-breaking state was, for understandable reasons, extremely prominent during the war and has

THE FELT NEED

sunk into deeper and deeper twilight ever since. To those who saw in the opening of the Great War, especially the invasion of Belgium, little more than a flagrant breach of international law, it was natural to conceive that the thing chiefly wanted for the general safety was a Sanction behind international law. Similarly, to those who, under the emotions of the time, saw the war as an outbreak of wickedness on the part of a nation which was scarcely quite human, the chief necessity seemed to be a league of the law-abiding nations to control the criminal ones. The idea is in itself sound. There ought to be some sanction behind international law, and the League of Nations is there to supply it. But the first attempts to formulate it were often extravagant. There were suggestions that all the laws of war should be suspended in operations against the law-breaker, and the newly discovered horrors of science diligently developed for deterrent purposes. One proposal, advocated by a distinguished publicist and preached far and wide in England and America, recommended the retention of the Allied armies almost as they stood, under the command of General Foch, in order to enforce instantly the decisions of strict world-justice, which were to be laid down, if I remember rightly, by a Jury of Twelve. What was to happen if General Foch did not agree with the Jury was not clearly stated. People at that time were still obsessed by military ideas, and did not realize the strong impulse felt in all countries to get away from the whole régime of war, and the extreme difficulty there would be afterwards in re-enacting any part of it. But the essential error of all these plans for building the peace of the world on a special army, or special weapons, or the like, is that they misconceive the problem. The problem is not how to concentrate somewhere sufficient force to quell a peace-breaker—that already exists; it is to produce a general state of mind in which the possessors of force will really use it for maintaining the general peace and not merely for supporting their own interests.

Another idea which was very popular among the reformers of 1917–1919 was the settlement of international differences by law. Some authorities believed that an International Court could be created which should settle all differences whatsoever. A very distinguished Professor of Law explained to me at this time that all that was wanted was an International Court and a strong military force to execute its decisions; the legal differences it could decide by law, the clashes of interest and prestige, and the like, it could settle by something like what in English law is called Equity, *ex æquo et bono*. There was no need for any other authority. The most usual proposal, however, was to divide disputes into two classes, the justiciable and the non-justiciable, those which were suitable for judicial decision and those that were not. The classes were for the most part not more closely defined, and the names by which they are called have varied since. The Covenant speaks of disputes "recognized as suitable for submission to arbitration or judicial decision"; the Treaty of Locarno describes them as disputes in which "the parties are in conflict as to their respective rights". The examples given are disputes as to the interpretation of a treaty, questions of international law, questions of fact and reparations for wrong done; but it seems clear that these four classes are not meant to be exhaustive. It would be unfortunate if they were.

Under the schemes put forth by Lord Bryce's committee, the League of Nations Society, and the American League to Enforce Peace, justiciable disputes were to be referred compulsorily to some judicial or arbitral tribunal, whose decision was to be accepted as final. The Hague Court of Arbitration was generally mentioned. This proposal has been in part realized, and in part improved upon, in the Covenant. But the non-justiciable disputes were under those schemes to be treated in a way quite different from that which was afterwards adopted.

The non-justiciable disputes, which were recognized as being probably the most numerous and certainly the most difficult, were to be referred to a Council of Conciliation. The constitution of this Council was left uncertain or defined in different ways: it was to be representative of all the nations in the League, but emphatically it was not to consist of members of the actual Governments. It was assumed that the

Governments had already got their nations into a mess and probably committed themselves to particular national views; so that fresh minds and clean hands were necessary. And besides, there was in most countries, as the war went on, a growing distrust of all national Governments. The Council of Conciliation was as a rule to have no executive power. It could merely issue reports or make recommendations, and very few schemes proposed to make the acceptance of these recommendations compulsory. The nearest approach to it perhaps was in Article XX of the Bryce scheme, directing that "if any Power shall fail to accept and give effect to the recommendations contained in any report of the Council (of Conciliation), the signatory Powers shall meet in Conference to consider . . . what collective action, if any, it is practicable to take in order to make such recommendations operative". This Council of Conciliation has disappeared from the horizon. It would have been, I think, a somewhat helpless body. No body which is not the Government can, except by revolution, supersede the Government. The only remains of it are the small Committees of Conciliation set up by special agreement between some Scandinavian and Central European states, and recommended in the "General Act" of 1928. These committees generally consist of three permanent foreign members, agreed to by both parties, *plus* one member appointed *ad hoc* by each of the contending states. They have no executive powers, but form an additional instrument in the machinery for conciliation set up by the League.

In general one can see, looking back, that the compulsory enforcement, by arms or otherwise, of international decisions, formed much too large an element in the earlier proposals for the elimination of war. The idea of force dominated men's imaginations. In the American proposals, for instance, the only occasions when a conference of the members of the League is contemplated are (1) the coercion by common action of a recalcitrant member and (2) the codification of international law. I am therefore the more pleased to see that the British League of Nations Society—one of the parents of our Union—put in the forefront of its proposals "conferences to consider international matters of a general character".

The truth is that both the military and the legal ideas were sound in principle; disputes ought to be settled by arbitration, and war ought to be absolutely prevented; but in the early discussions about the League we all took too lightly the difficulty of a frontal attack on the real wish of a sovereign state. The proposals which have ultimately proved most successful were far more modest.

The most successful of all has been that of Conference. If only nations would confer with one another, if they would form the habit of sitting round a table and discussing, they could avoid most of their conflicts. It was remembered that Sir Edward Grey had urged and almost besought the Central Powers to come to a Conference about the Serbian question; it was felt that the refusal of Germany to come to Conference was tantamount to refusing peace. Besides that, all through the war the Allies had formed the habit of Conference. They had learned to co-operate. No Great Power, indeed, had quite consented to allow itself to be outvoted by a majority: a sovereign independent state could hardly be as sensible as that; but they had learned to work the rule of unanimity, under which no one is outvoted, but everyone makes, or is ready to make, concessions. A paper drawn up by Lord Robert Cecil which was used by the Committee on Foreign Relations of the U.S. Senate in its first session on the Treaty of Peace with Germany well describes the proposed working of the League:—

> The treaty will explicitly provide for *regular conferences* between the responsible representatives of the contracting Powers. These conferences would review the general conditions of international relations and would naturally pay special attention to any difficulty which might seem to threaten the peace of the world. . . . These conferences would constitute the pivot of the League.
>
> For the conduct of its work the inter-state Conference will require *a permanent Secretariate*. The General Secretary should be appointed by the Great Powers, if possible choosing a national of some other country.

The Conferences *plus* the permanent Secretariate suffice to constitute the League, and make in themselves the chief correction that was immediately

THE FELT NEED

possible in the old international anarchy. As to the Conferences, it is noteworthy that Lord Robert's paper speaks of

> an annual meeting of the Prime Ministers and Foreign Secretaries of the Great Powers, and quadrennial meetings of representatives of all states included in the League.

As a matter of fact, the Conferences of the Council take place not once but four times a year at least, and the Assembly of the whole League not every four years but every year. That is to say, the Conferences have been found so useful that they are in practice convened four times as frequently as was planned.

As to the Secretariat, its importance is far greater than was ever anticipated, either in the various unofficial schemes for a League of Nations or, I think, in the actual debates at Versailles. The cardinal difference which it makes in world affairs is this, that it constitutes a great permanent staff of international officials, whose business is international co-operation and whose professional self-respect is wrapped up in the preservation of peace. As soon as a rift occurs, or is likely to occur, between two nations, whatever the national newspapers and politicians may do, the Secretariate, both consciously and unconsciously, is at work to heal it. There are sure to be on the Secretariate nationals of both the countries involved in the quarrel. There are many neutrals, always working towards making the disputants reasonable. These people know each other; they are familiar with the question at issue; they see one another's point of view and national interest. Together they try to find ways out of the trouble. And when the time arrives for the politicians to meet in conference, they generally find that the possibilities have been well studied and the atmosphere of peaceful settlement, if not the actual proposals, already prepared. How far this result is due to the remarkable gifts of Sir Eric Drummond and the skill with which he chose his original staff is not for me to estimate; nor yet how far the high international spirit of the Secretariate is likely to be compromised by the pressure of certain Governments to obtain posts for their own nominees and to exclude individuals who have offended, or by the increasing custom of manning the higher posts in the Secretariate with professional diplomats who intend after a few years to return to their own national services and who look to their own Governments for promotion. The one thing that seems clear is that the Secretariate ought to offer a career to a man of first-class ability, at least as permanent, as attractive, and as well-provided as any national Civil Service. This is a matter of cardinal importance. We want the very best men at Geneva, not the third best. An incompetent or disloyal Secretariate would absolutely wreck the League. As it is, the world cannot be too thankful for the existence of this great office, genuinely international in spirit, continuously at work, to which all international discord is a kind of disgrace and every honest reconciliation a professional triumph.

I consider, therefore, that, as Lord Robert Cecil explained in his paper, the system of Conference *plus* a permanent Secretariate is the real essence of the League. It not only produces the atmosphere in which the machinery of conciliation can work; it makes possible almost all the constructive and co-operative work of the League. At this moment we may be thinking most about such problems as Disarmament, the evacuation of the Rhineland, and Sanctions against the Aggressor. But, if the League is successful, those problems ought before very long to be settled and pass into the background; the activities that are bound to increase are those which now seem secondary and which short-sighted politicians are always trying to cripple and reduce. I mean those in which nations are working constructively for the common good and laying the foundations of international government, almost always by a system of Conferences *plus* a permanent Committee or Secretariate: the economic co-operation, the formation of international law, the co-operation against disease, the various humanitarian undertakings; the immense field of joint action that lies before the International Labour Organization; and perhaps in course of time the full development of the latent seeds of intellectual co-operation. The world teems with problems not yet ripe for the politicians, which can only be solved by hard study, and which need the collaboration of the best brains of many nations. All these great vistas open before us as soon as we understand how to exploit the possibilities of Conference *plus* Secretariate.

But the League has, after all, to prevent war, and if disputes are not to be settled by war there must be some other way of settling them. This machinery is the second constituent factor of the League. The division of disputes into Justiciable and Non-justiciable, though somewhat pedantic in sound and not always perfectly clear in practice, has been accepted by the Covenant. Not that members are compelled to accept arbitration or legal decision for their justiciable disputes; they are only invited to do so and provided with an International Court in case they wish to use it. But the distinction is recognized, and works increasingly in practice. "Disputes about rights" —to adopt the Locarno phrase—may suitably be settled by law; but all disputes whatever must at least be submitted to conciliation.

There has been much discussion about the comparative merits of these two forms of peaceful settlement—Law and Informal Agreement. When two nations are involved in a dispute that is "likely to lead to a rupture", is it better that they should be induced, informally, by whatever means tact or ingenuity may suggest, to come to some voluntary agreement, or that either the dispute as a whole or at least the legal element in it should be taken out of their hands and settled according

THE FELT NEED

to justice by a disinterested tribunal? Much is to be said for Conciliation. It is argued that, in private life, it is almost always better that disputants should, when possible, settle their differences out of court. The very fact that a legal decision carries compulsion may easily provoke resentment. A nation, like an individual, will often accept a compromise which it is admittedly free to reject, but will resent the same proposal if it comes in the form of a judicial sentence. "If I must I won't, but if I needn't I don't mind", is a state of feeling well known to all of us. Again, even when a dispute has for its centre a question of legal right, like the present long-dragging difference between Hungary and Rumania about the Hungarian optants, it may often happen that a purely legal decision will not get to the heart of the difficulty; how much better that the two parties should, if possible, be induced to cooperate in the solution of their difference! One must also remember that law is not always justice. In present circumstances, while international law is admittedly far from perfect, there is nevertheless no effective machinery for changing it. A domestic law, if found unsatisfactory, can be altered by an Act of Parliament; but there is no Parliament to correct an international law.

Thus there is a strong case to be made for the use of conciliation rather than arbitration or legal decision in the greater number of ordinary disputes. But it only holds good under certain conditions. All parties affected by the dispute should have a fair hearing; strong nations should not be allowed to conciliate one another, as they have often done in the past, by each acquiescing in the other's wrongdoing towards third parties. The conciliator should be strictly honest and not too anxious to please. The disputants should be more or less equal in strength and influence; and above all, the alternative in the background, supposing settlement is refused, should be as it is in private disputes, judicial decision and not war. Law may be imperfect; but for a weak nation in conflict with a strong there is no other hope of a just decision. As long as the matter is left in the sphere of "conciliation", with no appeal to law in the background, the strong Power has the issue in its own hands. It can simply refuse all terms until it gets what it wants, while the weak will accept almost any compromise rather than lose everything. This state of things is in practice modified by conscience, by the influence of public opinion in the rest of the world, by the knowledge that flagrant and repeated acts of rapacity would probably bring, even for the strongest Power, unpleasant consequences; but it remains generally true that, when a dispute comes before any diplomatic body—that is, a body which is out for the most convenient settlement rather than for justice—the Great Power may feel secure that its interests will not seriously suffer, the small Power may feel thankful if it gets part of its due. This fact explains why the framers of the Covenant and the Court Statute were not able to give the Court

THE FELT NEED

full compulsory jurisdiction. The Great Powers would not allow them to do so. The situation as they left it is that no injured nation has the right to sue another; no guilty nation need ever come into Court unless it wishes. The farthest they dared to go was, by means of the Optional Clause (Clause 36) of the Statute of the Court, to give an opportunity, or perhaps we may say an invitation, to all well-disposed nations to accept the full compulsory jurisdiction if they wished. It explains also why the small nations as a whole are so eager for the general acceptance of the Optional Clause and why Great Britain has for so many years opposed it. I believe the opposition to be thoroughly short-sighted. It is true that by agreeing beforehand to accept the decision of the Court in all legal disputes Great Britain would probably here and there lose some point which she need not have lost if she had kept out of Court; but such small losses would, in my judgment, be utterly outweighed by the immense general increase of security and contentment which would follow from the definite acceptance by all the leading nations of "the reign of law in the sphere of law". Conciliation would still remain the common method, and ordinary diplomatic negotiations commoner still. But if things came to the worst, the last resort would be Law and not Force.

A secondary question of some importance is the issue between Arbitration in the strict sense and Judicial Decision. Before the foundation of the International Court, if two nations wished to settle a dispute by the nearest approach possible to the rights of the case, the only method was arbitration. It is a complicated process. The parties first agree to arbitrate; they then agree on the arbitrators, generally arranging to have one judge each on the arbitral body, and find whether the arbitrators are willing to act; they then agree on the *compromis*, or the statement of the exact point at issue, always a difficult matter, because, of course, each party likes to state the issue in a way favourable to himself, and there are always disputes as to the matters to be included or excluded. On each of these problems there are opportunities for a breakdown, and consequently opportunities for evasion and unfair pressure. Lastly, the tribunal itself is often open to criticism, since the judges nominated by each of the disputants may sometimes feel themselves bound to safeguard their country's interests rather than to give an unbiased judgment. The tribunal has to be appointed *ad hoc*, with no previous tradition, no continuity, and no power of building up precedents: all which things, whether recognized in law or not, must always have an effect on the future judgments of any tribunal. It was clear, therefore, in 1918 that the existence of a regular permanent Court, if a method could be devised of creating one, would be a great advance. A permanent Court would act consistently and with authority, and could hardly avoid building up a

THE FELT NEED

series of judgments which would eventually tend to grow into an accepted system of international law.

The advantages of such a Court were admitted, but its formation seemed impossible. To begin with, every nation insisted on having a judge of its own nationality. To accept this principle would have made an unwieldy tribunal, with a good many incompetent members and with every judge, as it were, partially bribed in the interest of his own nation. The Great Powers would none of it. They preferred a good workable tribunal on which they were fully represented while the rest of the world took its chance. The small nations quite refused this. The riddle was eventually solved by a proposal of Mr. Elihu Root, originally suggested, I believe, by one of the law professors at Harvard. By this plan there are two separate, though simultaneous elections, one by the Council and one by the vote of the Assembly sitting without the Council. In order to be elected, each judge must obtain an absolute majority in both elections, thus proving that he has the confidence of the Great Powers of the Council and the small Powers of the Assembly as well. Such a plan had not been possible before the formation of the League, but became easy afterwards. The Court is a little slow and its proceedings a little expensive; but as a just and competent international tribunal it has a record of practically unqualified success. It has on occasion given decisions against Great Powers as well as for them, in a way which shows it to be above the commoner considerations of diplomacy; and more remarkable still, it has established so firm a professional sense of duty that individual judges have more than once given judgments against their own nations—notably a French judge against France. I need hardly add that, though the Court possesses no armed force whatever, every one of its decisions has so far been obeyed and executed without question.

But after all, the ultimate question had still to be faced, of coercing the peace-breaker. This is the third constituent factor of the League, and a necessity if the world is to be sure of peace. Every nation, after making its laws as perfect as it can, has to consider what to do if people break them. The international community, if one may now use such a term, was confronted after the Great War with the same problem. It was important first of all to arrange for conferences and secondly to make a good Covenant; but there remained the third problem—what should be done if, in spite of Conference and Covenant, some nation staked its fortune on war? After all, the Great War had begun with a flagrant breach of treaty.

The special difficulty of the international problem was that the evil to be prevented was war, and there seemed to be no way of preventing it except war. Yet the recent "war to end war" had not been such a success that people in general wanted to try it again. Furthermore, in some quarters, especially among the northern neutrals, it was strongly felt that the real way to make war impossible was to establish an atmosphere of serene and unbroken peace, peace as a matter of course, with the reverse possibility negligible. How could we do that if we were to be always talking of war and preparing for it?

From the first the nations broke into two groups on this all-important question. The French and Belgians took an opposed view to that of the northerners. The war had begun by the German violation of Belgian neutrality; the law-abiding nations of the world had joined together to coerce the German criminal and put down his crime. If the Kaiser had known at the outset that England, Italy, and America would come in against him, he would never have broken the peace. Let it therefore be made beyond all question clear to any future malefactor who meditates war for the sake of ambition that that path is closed. The whole world will be down upon him, and his crime will not profit him. Let the undertaking be perfectly explicit: let its operation be swift and overwhelming. Let no miserable considerations of commerce or convenience or private interest interfere with the discharge of a supreme international duty. If everyone is ready to act, there will be no need to act. If not, if there is vacillation and doubt and selfish pacifism in the members of the League, then the war-plotter will think he is safe and will make his spring. For once, they said, perhaps for the only time in history, there was truth in the "hoary sophism": *Si vis pacem para bellum.*

The case so stated is without doubt very strong. If it makes most of us feel uncomfortable, that is not because of what it says, but because of something it seems to imply. It is not merely that, after all, it is the peaceful mind that breeds peace, and not the warlike mind: that if we lay at all too much stress on the need of warlike preparations for quelling the peace-breaker, we find ourselves on a very slippery slope. But worse than that: these proposals are all made in a world which is half armed and half disarmed, and their authors often imply that peace depends on keeping up that state of affairs. If the good nations, who won the war, are always ready to prevent aggression, and the wicked nations who lost it are not allowed to arm, all will be well. The good must, of course, keep up their armies and navies. They must make alliances among themselves—all, no doubt, consistent with the Covenant, and only to operate in self-defence. And then they must make sure that the wicked do not make alliances too; and so on. It is all a perpetuation of war, not a planting of peace: a hardening in old error, not a change of heart. One of the most advanced French advocates of the League once said to me that the true guarantee of peace in Europe was a strong French Army and a strong British Navy. The sort of man who thinks that is the sort of man who ought never to be allowed to touch international affairs.

Remove that implication. Accept freely, and

put into practice, the principle of genuine and equal Disarmament, and then your preparation for Sanctions is perfectly right. To put crushing Sanctions in the hands of two particular Powers, or of an alliance of certain highly armed Powers, would be a crime against humanity. But when the Sanctions express genuinely the will of the community of nations, and nations whose armaments have been voluntarily reduced to the level of the Germans, the Scandinavians or the South Americans, then the Sanctions become both a safe and a necessary part of the Covenant, and the more certain they can be made, the better.

Certainly, the makers of the Covenant, like the devisers of the various unofficial schemes, accepted the duty of coercing the peace-breaker. Let us consider the question of method.

> The signatory Powers shall jointly use forthwith both their economic and military forces against any one of their number who goes to war or commits acts of hostility against another of the signatories before any question arising be submitted (to peaceful settlement).

That is the principle laid down before the war by the League to Enforce Peace. The British League of Nations Society goes further into detail. The members shall use their economic and military forces against one of their number who goes to war without submitting, etc.; they shall do the same against any non-member who attacks a member without submitting, etc.; and further, in the case of a member who, without actually going to war, does not "abide by the terms of his treaty", they will "unite in any action necessary" to ensure that he does. And this is, apart from minor refinements, the exact position taken up in the Covenant. (1) The League unites to coerce the war-maker; (2) it treats the non-member war-maker exactly as it treats the member; and (3) in the case of a member who merely disobeys some decision or fails to carry out some engagement, "the Council proposes what steps shall be taken to give effect thereto".

These three decisions are, I think, practically inevitable. It is essential to the idea of the League, as it is to that of any law-abiding society, that the community as a whole should be prepared to coerce any individual wrongdoer. Otherwise society would be always at the mercy of its wickedest members. Further, though certain critics have been much shocked at the idea of the League "interfering with states outside the League", it would be ridiculous to undertake to defend any member against unjust attack by other members, but to let non-members attack him as much as they like. One could not give to non-members the special privilege, denied to members, of making war with impunity. On the other hand, though the League as a whole must do its best to see that its decisions are obeyed, it would be very rash to use force as a remedy against anything short of war. To bring in war as a corrective to mere disobedience would be like burning your house down to get rid of black beetles.

The real difficulty of the situation lies in the practical working of the coercion. Let it be laid down that the League as a whole will take the necessary action, economic or military. Well and good; but the League is not a military or economic unit and possesses no central executive. It is a society of independent sovereign states, their independence somewhat modified by treaty obligations and a habit of regular conference, but none the less real. I doubt whether the League as a League could declare war or wage war. The force would have to be supplied by each state separately, of its own deliberate will. Furthermore, one cannot fairly urge that every member of the League is in duty bound to act in every case where coercion by the League is necessary. One cannot expect Siam or Canada to mobilize because one Balkan state attacks another. And if the duty is not incumbent on all members, who is to decide what members are to undertake it? The Council has no absolute authority. No nation will be eager to subject itself to the strain and sacrifice of coercive action unless its own interests are sharply involved. But the question is whether, in a world that increasingly detests war and mistrusts force as an instrument of international policy, the various national Parliaments or Governments will in general have sufficient loyalty to the League, sufficient public spirit and sense of reality, to be ready to face the prospect of war not in defence of their own frontiers or immediate national interests, but simply to maintain the peace of the world.

There is no perfect solution of this problem. There will be none until that distant day when the League may become an actual Federation with a federal force of its own. Till then we must be content with the principles laid down by the committee of jurists on Article XVI: The Council is to "recommend" what steps should be taken; the nations, "while attaching the utmost importance" to the recommendation, are not bound to obey it; they undertake, however, each "in the degree which is compatible with its geographical situation and its position with regard to armaments, to co-operate loyally and effectively in support of the Covenant of the League". (The words were first used in Article 11 of the rejected Geneva Protocol, but have been adopted in the Treaty of Locarno and may be regarded as fairly expressing the position.)

It was hoped at the time when the Covenant was being drawn up that an instrument of coercion had been discovered which would make fighting unnecessary. At that time the organization of the Blockade was so perfect that a decision of the Supreme Council of the Allies could within a few days subject any offending nation to a pressure gradual but eventually irresistible, working like a mediæval sentence of excommunication and interdict. It was, for the purpose of coercing a warmaker, an ideal weapon, a punishment exactly fitted to the crime. For the nation which reintroduced war for its own ambitions had *ipso facto* cut itself off from the society of the civilized world,

THE FELT NEED

and the world's natural answer would be, not to do business with it. It was also good because of its gradual action. The application of the boycott, gradually increasing to blockade, would show the offending nation what was coming, but would not produce immediate bloodshed or loss of life.

Yet it had a fatal, or almost fatal, defect. It needed unanimous action to be effective. To be entirely cut off from the rest of the world would be an irresistible penalty; to be cut off from some nations while free to trade with others would be a mere inconvenience. And, what was worse, the proclamation of a general boycott imposed a heavy sacrifice on all the honest nations which complied with it, and offered immense profits to any dishonest nation which did not comply. For example, if in 1923 the League had proclaimed a boycott against Italy on the Corfu question, Switzerland would have been in a difficult position. If she joined in the boycott, Ticino might be overrun by the Italian army; if she abstained from the boycott but continued to trade with Italy, she would acquire all the trade of her more conscientious neighbours, and her merchants would become most undeservedly rich. Lastly, the world organization for the control of trade which worked so well in 1918 had taken four years of war to build up; and it was found that the sacrifices it imposed on the boycotting nations, and the strictness of organization necessary for making the boycott effective, were so severe that nations could scarcely be expected to submit to them in times of peace. The problem of finding an instrument for coercing the wicked without imposing almost equal suffering and loss on the virtuous is still unsolved; that is, of course, if the wicked are at all powerful. The coercion of a weak malefactor has seldom presented much difficulty.

Attempts have been made to escape from the apparent ineffectiveness of these arrangements for coercive action against the war-maker. Two are worthy of special mention. In the present text of Article XVI it is laid down that "Should any member resort to war in disregard of his Covenants, it shall *ipso facto* be deemed to have committed an act of war against all other members of the League". That is, it has committed an act of war, and all other members have the right to take whatever action they think fit. They may make war or not make war. But an earlier form of the article used the much stronger term: "it shall *ipso facto* be deemed to be at war with all other members". The declaration of war was, so to speak, automatic; it was not a matter of choice. The provision was considered too strong, and the present formula substituted.

Again, in the Protocol of 1924 a vigorous effort was made to secure the complete abolition of war. The methods may be roughly summarized thus: (1) A definite agreement to abolish war; (2) the provision of compulsory arbitration for all disputes whatever in which voluntary agreement has failed; and (3) making the coercive action of the League prompt and certain. Under the Covenant in its present form it is for the Council to decide whether or no a particular war-making state has broken its Covenant and committed aggression. The states involved in the conflict do not vote, but the rest of the Council has to be unanimous. Consequently, it was justly argued, a deliberate war-maker has only to win one member of the Council to take its side and it can paralyse the League. The Council can take no unanimous decision and Article XVI will not operate.[1] The remedy for this flaw was sought in an attempt to make the test of aggression automatic. Any state which resorted to war in breach of its undertakings was an aggressor; the test was simply the striking of the first blow. If there was doubt about this first blow, the Council imposed an armistice on both parties, and any state which violated the armistice was the aggressor. The detailed provisions of the Protocol were considered to make the test automatically clear. The Council had merely to register the fact of aggression, and, in order to prevent any paralysis of its action by intrigue, no choice was left to it unless by a unanimous vote it should decide that the presumed aggressor was really not so.

The Protocol was certainly strong meat. Yet the states of Europe in general were ready to accept it. They are all prepared for heavy sacrifices

---

[1] This, of course, does not mean that individual members of the Council are debarred from acting. They would in most cases simply "recover their freedom", as the original war-maker had done.

in order to be really and completely saved from the danger of war. Germany and Hungary, it must always be remembered, welcomed the Protocol as warmly as France and Czechoslovakia. It was wrecked by the British Government, partly perhaps for party reasons, partly from a rooted and most mistaken reluctance to forgo its "right of war", but also from a correct estimate of the general feeling of the country. Apart from the ordinary instinctive desire to have peace and security, like other good things, without paying the price for them, and that reluctance to undertake any firm engagement concerning the future which has given England and America such a bad name in international negotiations, there was a genuine feeling throughout the country that the engagements were too tight, that no human power could foresee the possible contingencies, and that ultimately the Protocol might not only land Great Britain in war but might set her fighting against a "presumed aggressor" whom she really believed to be in the right. There was still too much mutual distrust in the nations of Europe. "Make a firm treaty and we can trust each other", said the French and those who thought with them; "we cannot trust you while you refuse to commit yourselves." "We will make a firm treaty when once we do trust each other", responded the British and Scandinavian elements; "we cannot pledge ourselves to you till we are sure that you are playing fair."

It is this kind of imperfection rather than any

actual incompleteness of provision or flaw of drafting that has most hampered the working of the League for peace. It can only be removed by a much more whole-hearted acceptance of the League spirit and League methods on the part of the Great Powers.

IV

THE WORLD INSIDE THE COVENANT: THE INTERNAL FLAWS

MOST penitence has its lapses. Mediæval stories tell us of passionately repentant murderers who became monks and rose to eminence by their austere and consistent piety. But it would be most unjust to compare the European nations or Governments to such criminals. Their sins were much less scarlet, and their repentance has been a half-hearted affair. When a great mass of men, such as constitute a modern nation, are committed by their leaders, under the influence of special circumstances and emotions, to a profound and permanent change of policy, it is quite impossible that the change should be clear-sighted, complete and free from inconsistencies. *"In the long run"*, says Bishop Gore with profound truth, *"what any society is to become will depend on what it believes or disbelieves about the eternal things."* But, after all, most members of most political societies think very little about the eternal things; very few know what they believe or disbelieve, or would be at all capable of putting the beliefs into words. The acceptance of the Covenant of the League did imply on the part of all the signatory states, but for some much more than others, a great *Metanoia*, a change of mind or heart: and naturally they do not always find themselves capable of living up to it. Even in England, where the old tradition was comparatively innocent, and where League education has been more active and successful than elsewhere, you may hear people in the train making forecasts about "the next war", and gossiping about supposed "secret treaties" and secret weapons, and espionage and the stealing of diplomatic documents, without any consciousness that they are accusing His Majesty's Government of perjury. And in some other countries it is much worse. In Italy important governmental newspapers write of the Kellogg Peace Pact as a piece of obvious hypocrisy; Italy has signed it, for reasons of politeness, but will, of course, make war when opportunity occurs "to guarantee her right to life and a future".[1]

Hungarian officials in responsible positions speak with enthusiasm of a war to recover their lost territory, and Polish officers of wars to right and left to make Poland "safe". Those countries have their dangers. It is stranger to hear sober Americans, when not a tomtit in the wide universe utters a chirp to threaten their security, talk glibly of the need of a vast navy to make themselves "respected" and the need of inventing synthetic rubber for the "inevitable war

[1] The *Popolo d'Italia*, postulating that in international relations there exists no law, admits that the stronger nations have every right, by means of a so-called "Pact to end War", to order lesser Powers to keep the peace. Italy by signing the Pact merely recognizes "a reality for the time being immutable". According to S. Alfredo Signoretti in the *Lavoro d'Italia*, there is among the signatories to the Pact "one great absentee: Italy's soul is not behind her signature . . . The ceremony of the signing of the Kellogg Pact is also its burial".—(*The Times*, September 21, 25, 28, 1928.)

with Europe". These things move one not so much to indignation as to a sort of despair of the human race. Certainly if these people are in their right minds and possess any practical sense of fact, the present civilization is doomed to a hideous end, and will richly deserve what it gets. But we must remember that such talk is not closely concerned with fact. Nine-tenths of it is the chatter of irresponsible outsiders, not the serious conversation of the Foreign Offices. It is largely the survival of an old habit, existing for countless ages and intensified by the recent war, in circumstances for which it is no longer suitable. I remember reading of an old gentleman in the eighteenth century who had the habit of emphasizing his remarks by slapping the place where his sword-handle used to be when swords were still worn. It is also, no doubt, an expression of conscious or subconscious resentment against the League and all its implications. It is hard on many people, on naval and military circles, on Philistine newspapers, on smart society in London, just as it is hard on similar circles in Berlin, to have to give up their favourite dreams and admit themselves definitely defeated, defeated even in the Tory Cabinet, by dull middle-class pacifism. Since they cannot overthrow the new order, they like to pretend it is not there. When one reads the London Press or listens to the talk of an average club or drawing-room, one wonders how on earth the Covenant was ever signed, since everyone seems to dislike and ignore it. Then you have to think again, and reflect that all parties are pledged to the League: that all Prime Ministers and ex-Prime Ministers support it: that no candidate for Parliament dares to oppose it openly. I think the explanation is that in England the social system is still aristocratic while the political is democratic. The so-called Conservatism of smart clubs and drawing-rooms is quite different from Conservatism in Parliament, and it is Parliament that counts. Consequently, I am not much moved by the talk of secret alliances and next wars. If anyone will put himself imaginatively in the position of a German or Hungarian or Italian nationalist, bent on plunging his country into a bloody adventure to recover its "rights", and consider the practical difficulties confronting him, I think he will presently convince himself that—unless some quite unforeseen catastrophe should alter all the conditions—the enterprise of the war-maker in present-day Europe is flatly unworkable. As a matter of fact, almost all the nationalist parties have already seen it, and accepted, with good grace or bad, the Stresemann-Briand policy.

The danger, however, is not direct war-making. It hardly ever has been. When the Prime Minister, on October 26, 1928, in a speech for which the L.N.U., the Conservative Party, and the whole nation owe him real gratitude, made certain severe remarks about the tiger within us, I felt that I was hearing a dumb animal ill spoken of behind its back. I do not believe that the tiger has anything appreciable to do with the bringing

INSIDE THE COVENANT

on of war. He arrives on the scene after the war has started, and then, of course, he makes us all tigrish; but he does not bring the war on. War in modern conditions is never a mere outburst of angry passions; it is simply the result of bad policy—stupid, selfish, narrow-minded, aggressive or dishonest policy. It is perfectly futile for any statesman or any citizen, standing before the tribunal of history to say: "I never wanted war. I dislike war extremely." Men do not go to prison because they like prison: they do not have *delirium tremens* because they have a taste for *delirium tremens*. Governments find themselves at war, not because they like war, but because, in spite of all experiences and all admonitions, they go on doing the things that lead to war. They have had their lesson but not learnt it. They drift on, behaving in the ways in which they have always behaved. It is by that, when the time comes, that they will stand condemned. It is perfectly true that, as the Prime Minister said with much eloquence, there is generally behind these bad policies a touch of the tiger-spirit in reserve. The tiger is there, and we must keep him down by prayer and fasting, by thinking twice and thrice before we set out to denounce other nations or malign our political opponents, or to encourage the military spirit of the nation by the methods of the fraudulent advertiser. But it is most important to realize that "tigrishness" is not the main danger. The danger is that from ordinary inertia and reluctance to think hard, and perhaps also from undue familiarity with evasive formulæ, the Governments will all go on behaving in ways that are inconsistent with peace. The true way to peace is by a conscientious execution of the Covenant:—

> By the acceptance of obligations not to resort to war;
> by . . . open, just and honourable dealings between nations;
> by the firm establishment of the understandings of international law as the actual rule of conduct among Governments; and
> by the maintenance of justice and a scrupulous respect for all treaty obligations in the dealings of organized peoples with one another.

And the trouble is that most nations, both great and small, think they can maintain peace otherwise.

The most obvious test is reduction of armaments. They have undertaken "to give their sincere co-operation to" the "Reduction and Limitation of Armaments by International Agreement", to deal with the "evils attendant on the private manufacture of arms", and "to interchange full and frank information about their armaments, their programmes, and those industries which are adaptable to warlike purposes".

This undertaking has proved difficult to carry out. One cannot perhaps convict any of the chief nations of actual breach of faith; but disarmament

INSIDE THE COVENANT 105

is not popular and no Government has tried very hard to fulfil its treaty. The conferences have one and all broken down on points which could have been overcome if Governments as a whole had felt at all as Lord Cecil or M. de Brouckère did. The various fighting departments absolutely refuse to exchange "full and frank information"; and no Government dares to coerce its fighting departments. Shameful to relate, they still prefer to get their information by mutual espionage. Nothing has as yet been accomplished about the control of private manufacture.[1] There are real difficulties in the problem, and meantime the private firms have great electoral influence and employ large numbers of men.

It might well seem to an observer curious that in the face of such obviously strong reasons for reducing armaments by international agreement they are still not reduced. There is the direct treaty obligation; there is the promise by which the Germans were induced to disarm, bearing in most people's eyes a rather special sanctity; there are the pressing calls for economy, and the obvious dangers of unilateral reduction; and there is the more remote but equally real danger that the only

[1] A Convention for the Control of the Traffic in Arms (owing much to the initiative of the British Delegate, Major Hills) was signed in 1925, and will be in force when ratified by fourteen Powers. It has so far been ratified by China, France, Holland, Venezuela; adhered to by Liberia. The Control of Private Manufacture has been "studied", and is to be studied further, by the Preparatory Commission.—The Exchange of Information on Armaments has been referred, on the motion of Count Bernstorff, to the same Commission. A pretty poor result for ten years!

alternative to an agreed reduction is a competitive increase, such as led to war in 1914 and must, as far as one can see, inevitably lead again to war. I think, apart from many difficulties of detail, the essential obstacle to agreed Disarmament has been, first, the natural resistance of the fighting departments, who instinctively give to all plans for disarmament much the same degree of "loyal and effective co-operation" as a dog gives towards the muzzling order; and secondly, in the ordinary civilian population, the ingrained and often unreasoning fear of war. It stands to reason that a nation which is genuinely afraid that it may be attacked will not agree to reduce its armaments. It would be foolish if it did. If we ask the reasons why any nations are still afraid, they fall under two heads.

First, there is the imperfection of the treaties. There is the gap in the Covenant, still permitting war in any dispute over which the Council is not unanimous, and there are the many uncertainties affecting sanctions against the war-maker. War can still be made, and there is no certainty that the nation attacked will be defended by the rest of the League. The advocates of the Protocol and the Treaty of Mutual Assistance argue with much force that these dangers are easy to remedy if only the Great Powers would accept their due responsibilities. But at present they will not. Next, the imperfections of the international atmosphere. "It is not the treaties that make the trouble", say opponents of any change in the Covenant, "it is

INSIDE THE COVENANT 107

the lack of 'moral disarmament' in the minds of the nations themselves. The treaties will do well enough when once there is real change of heart. Till then, it is no good tightening them." Meantime Disarmament Conferences hang fire, and it is not, I think, cynical to remark that the average citizen is rather relieved that they do. He would be sorry to lose his big guns and battleships, which minister to his self-respect in much the same way as his new golf-clubs and motor-car.

Let us consider, therefore, the fortunes of those articles in the Covenant which are specially concerned with the prevention of war: Article XVI binding members to take common action to coerce the war-maker, X depriving him of any gains he may acquire by his aggression, and XI declaring that any war or threat of war is a matter of concern to the whole League, and that "the League shall take any action that may be deemed wise and effectual to safeguard the peace".

On several occasions this pledge has been admirably carried out. The invasion of Albania by the Jugoslavs in 1922 was instantly stopped, and the evacuation of the country enforced in nine days. The war between Poland and Lithuania was stopped, though the dispute was never settled. The invasion of Bulgaria by Greece in 1925 was stopped by telegram, the whole dispute inquired into and reparations loyally paid. There are some other cases almost as striking.

On the other hand, there are cases where the

Council of the League, if it had simply stood by its pledges and done its duty, could have acted effectively, instead of which it broke into groups, influenced by their supposed diplomatic interests, and was paralysed. When Poland attacked Russia in 1920, the League was divided and said nothing. When General Zeligowski, by a surprise attack, took Vilna from the Lithuanians, it was just the same. The Council, in order to avoid trouble, acquiesced in an obviously wrong action, and consequently has had infinite trouble with Lithuania ever since. Lithuania will still not trust the League, because the League once failed in its duty. When Italy in 1923 bombarded and seized Corfu, the Council was weak and divided; it was only the firmness of Lord Robert Cecil, supported by all the small nations of the Assembly, which brought about the restoration of the island and the reference of the dispute to peaceful settlement. The weakness of that settlement in detail was due immediately to the Conference of Ambassadors; but behind the weakness of the Ambassadors was the weakness of the Council, and behind both the unconscientiousness of the Governments themselves.

In these cases there was no very formidable obstacle to correct action. A unanimous Council could have carried out its obligations without danger. On the other hand, it is important to realize that there may be cases where even a unanimous Council could not wisely act. It looked at one time as if the United States might be about to do violence to the "integrity and independence" of Panama, a member of the League; but it would clearly have been impossible for the League to defend its injured member or to bring the United States before any international tribunal. It would have had to act under Article XI and "safeguard the peace of nations" as best it could.

Such a situation produces the usual charges and counter-charges. "The pledges are too vague", say the French; "let us make them absolute and definite." "How can we do that?" reply the British, "when we see that you shrink from carrying out even the present pledges?" "With a firm agreement", retort the French, "we will act firmly. We cannot take risks while you expressly reserve the right to let us down." On such terms the dispute is insoluble; a little more conscientious loyalty to the Covenant on both sides and the difficulty would dwindle away.

There is something characteristic in the British policy of accepting Article XVI while refusing to say exactly what it means and reserving a full right to nullify it in action. The British people, accustomed to centuries of isolation, does, I fear, dislike being bound by any treaty. Besides, such a policy suits the party organizer. It saves the Government from the danger of ever having to take an unpopular course on grounds of honour and the pledged word. But it is the sort of policy that wrecks confidence abroad, and wins for our simple-minded statesmen a reputation for perfidious subtlety.

Again and again one hears in England, and not from one party only, the argument that the Rhine frontier is a "British interest"—that is supposed to have been shown by the Great War—but that the frontier of Poland or Bulgaria is not a British interest. The conclusion drawn is that the Treaty of Locarno is prudent and wise, because it only "guarantees the Rhine frontier", but that the full execution of Article XVI is impossible because that would involve "guaranteeing" all sorts of other "frontiers". Such talk is a good instance of thinking in obsolete terms. What Article XVI guarantees is not any frontier, but the public peace. The Polish frontier may be open to much criticism; the Poles drew it about a hundred miles farther to the east than Lord Curzon approved, and it would be absurd to claim that Great Britain must permanently uphold a frontier which the British Foreign Office has always considered wrong. We may hope that in course of time it will be altered; but, if the Covenant is to stand, it must not be altered by violence. No Power henceforth may take the law into its own hands. That is what the members of the League are solemnly pledged to prevent. It is a matter of duty, not of interest. If each Great Power is to be free, in each case, to consider whether it suits its own interest to join in action against the aggressor, or whether it would be cheaper and more popular to sit still, there is not much of the Covenant left. The whole force of Article XVI is that the members of the League pledge themselves to take certain action for the sake of the League, irrespective of their own preferences. Thus the juridical obligation is both important and clear. But the practical necessity is hardly less so. It is surely pretty certain, for example, that if the Bolshevik Government of Russia began a career of westward conquest by invading Poland, or if the Fascist Government of Italy started a career of northward conquest in Croatia and Austria, the League would receive just as great a shock as if war broke out between France and Germany. It is an obsolete habit of thought which imagines that Great Britain can sit still and let the nations of Eastern Europe fight as they will. "Any war or threat of war, whether immediately affecting any member of the League or not, is a matter of concern to the whole League." It is a blunder in practical politics, as well as a breach of honour, for any Great Power to evade its obligation under Article XVI to join with the rest of the League in preventing aggression on the ground that the aggression in question does not affect its own interests. It does.

The legitimate limitations on League action under Article XVI are fairly obvious and have been laid down in the official commentaries. (1) It is clear that not every state is either bound or expected to take action; they should all in some degree share expenses, and take their part in the boycott, but only certain particular states whose "geographical position" and "situation as regards armaments" made them able to act easily and effectively should undertake the actual fighting. No doubt Great Britain and France, in view of their leading position and world-wide interests, would most often be called upon, while Italy and Japan, Poland and Jugoslavia, would pretty certainly not wish to be left out. (2) Certain states may claim a special exemption from the duty of taking part in coercive measures, if for some special reason the danger in which such action would involve them would be unduly great. The Council could hardly insist that Finland should blockade Russia, because Russia would eat her up if she did. They can hardly keep Germany disarmed with one hand and with the other compel her to fight. (3) The Council itself has a great responsibility. It does not by any means act automatically, nor does it wait for war to break out. It has presumably been acting, ever since the first suggestion of danger, under Article XI, taking whatever steps seemed wise and effectual to safeguard the peace of nations; and one of those steps has presumably been to impress on the would-be war-maker that the League will not allow him to make war. If he does, the League has nearly failed, but not quite, and the Council has to consider on practical grounds whether or no a call to action should be sent round to members of the League. Next, it has to consider the date at which it considers that such action—economic or military—ought to be taken. It can reserve this weapon as long as it thinks fit, and try in the meantime other methods of restoring the peace. For all the time it is bound by Article XI not to act in a blind mechanical way, but to take whatever action "may be deemed wise and effectual" to safeguard, or at worst to restore, the peace of nations. It will be influenced both by the readiness or unreadiness to act which it finds in its principal members, and by the probable size and difficulty of the conflict which its action will provoke. When the Russians, for example, destroyed the Georgian Republic, in circumstances of great cruelty, the League was not bound to act, because Georgia was not a member; but even if she had been, the Council might reasonably have argued that to start a war of Europe against Russia in order to prevent the oppression of Georgia would be to cure a smaller evil by a much greater one. Such a decision would perhaps be a tragic confession of weakness, but the weakness is, after all, a fact and may have to be confessed. (4) Lastly, there is the point we have elaborated above: that no state can be ordered by the Council of the League to make war or to enter on a boycott or blockade which may lead to war. It has to act by its own will, shown in whatever way its constitution requires. All it can promise is to "co-operate loyally and effectively" and to "attach high importance" to the recommendation of the Council. The agreements are certainly not water-tight. They offer many loopholes of escape to those who wish to evade their responsibilities. But given a fair standard of good faith in the Great Powers, I believe Articles XI and XVI should work effectively.

This brings us to another of the chief obstacles to vigorous action by members of the League. In the case of disputes such action would normally be in support of international law, and therefore of the *status quo*. International law is based partly on principles and precedents, partly on definite treaties; and the trouble is that neither the principles and precedents nor yet the Peace Treaties of 1919 are so perfect that they ought to remain for ever unchanged. Consider especially the treaties. To some nations of Europe, of course, the Peace Treaties are like holy writ. To Poland and Czechoslovakia and the Baltic Republics the treaties form the foundation of their existence as free nations; to Jugoslavia and Rumania they are the guarantee of their increased territories and their freedom from the domination of intriguing neighbours. Consequently these nations, with France as their leader, are in general ready at a moment's notice to fight on behalf of the treaties against any disturber of the peace. But the rest of Europe feels quite differently. The defeated nations regard the settlement as generally iniquitous; Great Britain and the neutrals regard it as on the whole an improvement on the previous arrangements, inasmuch as it pays far more regard to nationality, but they consider the financial clauses to be demonstrably oppressive and unworkable, while the territorial clauses are heavily loaded against the defeated nations. To British and neutral opinion, as a general rule, it seems clear that the treaties ought at some time or other to be reconsidered. It is impracticable to have them reconsidered now; impracticable as long as war is still a danger on the horizon. For no nation will give up any strategical advantage it possesses in territory or population as long as it thinks in terms of war. Thus the present frontiers and treaty settlements must be accepted for the time being: but it is too much—so British and neutral opinion will generally run—it is too much to ask us to undertake an obligation to use force or an economic blockade in order to perpetuate them.

The objection sounds reasonable, and there is only one motive that can be urged against it; but that is, I venture to think, a decisive one. It is more important to get rid of war than to rectify the treaties, and any nation which attempts to win its ends by war—and war contrary to its covenants—must be treated as an enemy of civilization. This is the great central principle of the League. One can strengthen it by other considerations: it is certain, for instance, that, if real justice and not revenge is our object, to attempt to remedy the defects of the treaties by war would be mere madness. No war can ever produce a just settlement. War is always and inevitably unjust to the vanquished; and a new war, whichever side won, would probably lead to a worse settlement than the last, because there would be no President Wilson trying, however ineffectively, to prevent injustice. Again, if it is really hoped to get a change in the settlement through diplomatic action, by persuading the present possessors to give up some of their alien territories and unwilling subjects, the only possible way to do so is by removing all danger of war. We must also remember that when once that is achieved some changes of frontier which now seem desirable may be so no longer. The remedy may be found in some other way; best of all, for instance, by simply making frontiers unimportant. If the League could bring about a state of things in which it mattered as little to a Pole or German, to a Magyar or a Rumanian, on which side of the frontier he lived, as it now matters to a citizen of Berwick-on-Tweed whether he is in England or Scotland, most of the evils of Europe would be healed forthwith.

In a paper drafted by Lord Robert Cecil in 1916 and presented to the Foreign Office the proposal was made that the territorial arrangements to be embodied in the Peace Treaties should "remain unaltered for the next five years. At the end of that period . . . a Conference of the High Contracting Powers shall be summoned, and any rearrangements of territory which have become necessary or desirable shall be then considered, and, if agreed upon, shall be forthwith carried out". The proposal was very likely not practicable. It might have led to all kinds of malpractices in the debatable areas, from fraudulent registers to actual massacre, just as agreements to hold future plebiscites have sometimes done. Its linear successor apparently was Article XIX of the

Covenant, enacting that "The Assembly may from time to time advise the reconsideration of treaties which have become inapplicable and the consideration of international conditions whose continuance might endanger the peace of the world". The Article is only permissive. There is no obligation, and the permission does not go far. The Assembly may, of course, only advise "reconsideration" or "consideration"; it cannot insist on alteration. And no use whatever, we must admit, has yet been made of the permission. That also must wait till peace is more secure. But the existence of this Article must never be forgotten; and its full development into practical effectiveness is, in my opinion, a vital necessity to the future of the League. Unless Article XIX can be made practically effective, the League will break. Meantime, the nations suffering from injustices must continue to suffer until it is clear that they are not thinking of redressing their grievances by war.

So be it. Yet those nations have in other ways a serious complaint to make. "If you will not modify the peace settlement," they may say, "even where the public opinion of the world thinks it ought to be modified, you might at least carry out the few clauses in the Peace Treaties which were designed in our favour as well as the many which bear hard against us."

It will be said, no doubt, that no one with a moderate knowledge of history and of human nature can be surprised that after so bitter a war the beaten party was subjected to a good deal of hard treatment. But that plea is hardly fair. The League was created expressly to prevent this injustice and persecution. The Covenant was to mark the great Repentance. And the trouble is that the League itself was composed at first entirely of victors and neutrals, and the voice of the victors has still a dominating influence. Few would deny that for some years at any rate almost every doubtful point which came before the Council was decided with a bias against the Germans. The repeated invasions of German territory, beginning with the occupation of Ruhrort Duisberg and Düsseldorf, in March 1921, and culminating with that of the Ruhr in January 1923, were by no means certainly consonant with the treaty. Most English authorities considered them illegal; but when the German Government made an application to the League to have the issue tried, the Council took no notice of the application. That is, the League acquiesced in proceedings of doubtful legality for no very visible reason except that the French insisted. The plebiscite in Eupen and Malmedy was openly flouted; the plebiscite in Upper Silesia was managed on a highly complicated principle which resulted in giving much advantage to Poland. The administration of the Saar territory by a Commission under the League became from time to time something like an open scandal. Not that there was oppression: quite the reverse. There was too much anxiety to win votes in the future plebiscite. But the Commission, which by constitution was to be strictly impartial, was in practice overpoweringly French. It was only after several years that the Council gradually succeeded in getting the terms of the treaty fairly observed. Later on, in the ordinary course of diplomacy, most critics will admit that an extreme deference is generally paid to the wishes or convenience of France, Italy, and Great Britain, while in any difference between Poland and Germany, Rumania and Hungary, Jugoslavia and Bulgaria, the first named receive a degree of consideration denied to their neighbours. It is possible that the outside critic is here making a harder demand than he realizes. There has been no real scandal, and it is perhaps an impossible thing to alter the ordinary well-established methods of diplomatic give-and-take wherever they are not perfectly honest. Still, an Englishman might have hoped that Great Britain would have been more vigorous in the part of honest arbiter. At one time she was so. As it is, there has been at times some justification for the Geneva epigram, "England expects every Swede to do her duty".

More continuous injustice and danger is involved in the problem of Minorities. At the end of the war the victorious Powers had called into existence the new states of Poland and Czechoslovakia and greatly increased the territories of other states. In every case there had been assigned to these states a large population alien in language, race, and religion. These alien minorities were thus placed under the rule of those from whom they were estranged by generations of enmity and in some cases by recent internecine warfare. The statesmen of Versailles realized that in such conditions there was certain to be persecution, and that in such persecution would be a seed of future war. The subject minorities in Europe before the war were more numerous than now, but the exasperation was not so great, the oppression more chronic than acute. The minorities are now said to amount in all to between thirty and forty millions. If so large a number were either goaded to desperation or taught to look for protection to their kindred in foreign states, the danger to European peace would obviously be very real. To avoid this danger, the recognition of the new states was made dependent on certain conditions similar to those imposed in the nineteenth century on various Balkan nations liberated from Turkey: members of racial, religious, or linguistic minorities were to have the same treatment and security in law and in fact as other nationals. They should be allowed to use their own language in courts of law, and on certain conditions in elementary schools. They should have a right to establish, manage and control at their own expense charitable religious and social institutions, schools, etc. The duty of seeing that these clauses were observed was by treaty entrusted to the Council of the League. Any member of the Council has a right to bring before that body any infraction, or any danger of infraction, of the regulations, and the Council may thereupon take such action as it deems proper.

These were admirable provisions. The objection that they put the new states in a position of inferiority or of incomplete sovereignty was partly met by a Resolution of the Fourth Assembly (1923) expressing the unanimous hope that the nations not bound by Minority Treaties would treat their own minorities at least as well as if they were. Such a "hope" is not binding: but the Resolution gives to any Delegate at the Assembly the right to ask why some particular Great Power is not fulfilling the "hope" it once expressed and how it explains certain facts.

It is a tragic commentary on the way in which the Council has performed its duties under these treaties that a leading member of the Council, speaking at a luncheon in Geneva in 1928, said it would perhaps have been better if the treaties had never been made and the minorities merely been left at the mercy of their alien rulers. The League procedure has been slow and half-hearted. To judge from the cases published, a petition on behalf of a minority, which is, of course, sometimes a matter of urgency, takes about a year to come before the Council. A very large number of petitions, proper and improper, are, or at least used to be, sent in; but few reach the Council at all. In almost no case has effective action been taken. In only two has the Council sent a question of law on to the International Court, and those both occurred during the short period when Lord Cecil sat on the Committee of Three. The influence of the League has been exercised almost entirely in one way: through personal visits paid to the Governments by members of the Minorities Section of the Secretariate. The truth is that the method provided by the treaties, viz. the raising of the alleged grievance as a "dispute" before the Council under Article XV of the Covenant, the parties to the dispute being the impugned Government and some member of the Council, is too ponderous and invidious to be often applied. No Allied Government, when its own interests are not concerned, likes to take upon itself a "dispute" with an ex-ally, who is perhaps a colleague on the Council, on behalf of an utterly weak and unpopular body of ex-enemies. The chief use of the procedure has been as a threat in the background. The official paying his friendly and private visit to some impugned Government can always suggest that, if no change is made, the Council will be compelled to take action. It is difficult to estimate the practical success which has attended these visits. The proceedings have to be confidential; to publish results would be to "blacken the face" of Governments. For the same reason, visits are seldom or never paid to the only persons who could give full information, viz. members of the aggrieved minority itself. To do so would be to offend the Government and make trouble for the people visited. My impression, which may well be mistaken, is that during the early years of the League, when there was a constant stir in the

Assembly about the treatment of minorities and action by the Council seemed to be a real possibility, the visits of the Secretariate had considerable effect, but that in the last few years the Governments have ceased to fear the Council and consequently have given up paying much attention to the polite remonstrances of the Secretariate. In those countries where the alien minority is rich and strong, like the German minority in Czechoslovakia, or where the various different minorities can unite for electoral purposes, as sometimes in Poland, they have largely succeeded in looking after themselves. It is where they are helpless of themselves that the Council ought to have protected them and has not. In Macedonia a boy may be beaten or have his face torn with a curry-comb by his Serbian or Greek schoolmaster for speaking with a Bulgarian accent, but his father, if he values life and limb, will not let the League hear of it. Bulgarian farmers may be terrorized out of Greece to make room for the Greek refugees from Asia Minor. Whole masses of unfortunate people—there are said to be over 30,000 in Rumania alone—may be deprived by chicane of all nationality and all political rights, forbidden to cross any frontier and forbidden to reside where they are except on payment of bribes. The Germans have not yet thought it wise to bring such cases before the Council. The French do not believe in championing ex-enemies against ex-allies. The British say that the important thing is to keep on good terms with the other Great Powers, and that to mention minorities produces an irritable atmosphere.

The question of Minorities is surrounded by difficulties. That must be admitted. It is easy to charge the minorities with disloyalty; in a sense the charge is always true, and the worse you treat them, the more true it becomes. I made at the Assembly of 1923 a proposal which I still think would have gone far to prevent the worst persecutions on the one hand and the alleged conspiracies on the other. It was to have in the most troubled districts resident Agents or Consuls of the League to observe and report and act as peacemakers. That proposal failed. But anyone who looks back to the treaties and the communications accompanying them, to Mr. Wilson's speech and M. Clemenceau's famous letter, can hardly help feeling that a more courageous and conscientious spirit in the Council of the League would have lessened, and not increased, the difficulties.[1] As

[1] President Wilson drew attention to the responsibility which rested ultimately upon the Great Powers for maintaining the peace settlement. He continued: "In those circumstances is it unreasonable and unjust that, not as dictators but as friends, the Great Powers should say to their associates: 'We cannot afford to guarantee territorial settlements which we do not believe to be right, and we cannot agree to leave elements of disturbance unremoved which we believe will disturb the peace of the world.' Take the rights of minorities. Nothing, I venture to say, is more likely to disturb the peace of the world than the treatment which might in certain circumstances be meted out to minorities. And therefore, if the Great Powers are to guarantee the peace of the world in any sense, is it unjust that they should be satisfied that the proper and necessary guarantee has been given?" (Speech at the Plenary Session of the Peace Conference, May 31, 1919.)

M. Clemenceau wrote: "The Principal Allied and Associated Powers are of opinion that they would be false to the responsibility

it is, the dangers to European peace remain festering.

The neglect of the minorities cannot but suggest to the mind a serious criticism on modern democratic government as a whole. A decent autocracy or a governing class does realize, to some extent, that it has a duty to see to the welfare of the voteless and powerless masses for whom it

which rests upon them if on this occasion they departed from what has become an established tradition. In this connection I must also recall to your consideration the fact that it is to the endeavours and sacrifices of the Powers in whose name I am addressing you that the Polish nation owes the recovery of its independence. It is by their decision that Polish sovereignty is being re-established over the territories in question and that the inhabitants of these territories are being incorporated in the Polish nation. It is on the support which the resources of these Powers will afford to the League of Nations that for the future Poland will to a large extent depend for the secure possession of these territories. There rests, therefore, upon these Powers an obligation, which they cannot evade, to secure in the most permanent and solemn form guarantees for certain essential rights which will afford to the inhabitants the necessary protection whatever changes may take place in the internal constitution of the Polish State." (Letter addressed to M. Paderewski when the Treaty of Peace with Poland was submitted to him, June 24, 1919.)

At the Assembly of 1928 M. Beelaerts van Blokland (Netherlands) recalled the proposal made at the Second Assembly, and again urged this year by the International Federation of L.N. Societies, to create a Permanent Minorities Commission. "The present Minorities Committee met during the session of the Council at a time when all the members of Council were overwhelmed with work, so that they were not always able to attend the Committees in person. This was hardly satisfactory from the point of view of the responsibilities of the Committee towards the Council. Further, it was difficult for a member of the Council to be sure whether the grounds of a petition were good or bad, notwithstanding the very clear and helpful memoranda supplied by the Minorities Section. He asked the delegates to consider whether the best way of remedying these defects would not be to set up a Permanent Minorities Commission, similar to the Permanent Mandates Commission." At the meeting of September 8th M. Motta (Switzerland) supported this proposal.

is responsible. But democracies depend entirely on the system of representation; the security which democracy provides is that every class by means of its vote can look after itself. If it is oppressed, it can make its voice heard, and may turn out the Government. Consequently, Governments form the habit of attending sympathetically to the complaints of every class that can really make trouble and ignoring those who cannot. If the sort of things done to aliens in British and American ports were ever done to British or American citizens, there would be an outcry; and the Governments would censure their agents or mend their ways. But foreigners have no votes, so it does not matter what is done to them. In the same way, each member of the Council feels that the good will of the other Powers is of great value to him; the feelings of ignorant peasants in Macedonia or "stateless" outcasts in Rumania are of no value at all. And to attend to things of no value is not politics.

There is also another class of human beings, numbered by many millions, whose feelings are of no particular importance to anybody, while the people with whom they come into conflict are just those whom European Governments, including even the British, are very reluctant to offend. If one looks through recent human history, apart from the Great War, and tries to collect the very worst abominations perpetrated by man upon man, he will find them, I think, in places where a ruling race, for whatever motive, was working its

INSIDE THE COVENANT

will on a subject race: the Armenian massacres, the abominations of the Congo rubber-monopoly, the still darker horrors of the Putumayo. Those are fortunately very exceptional cases, but the problem which they illustrate is common. As long as great inequalities exist between different races of men, so long in some form or other the principle of Empire will exist; and these proceedings are the darkest side of Empire. There are, as a matter of fact, "peoples not yet able to stand by themselves under the strenuous conditions of the modern world", and the Covenant lays down for the League "the principle that the well-being and development of such peoples form a sacred trust of civilization". Securities for the performance of this trust are therefore embodied in the Covenant.

The sincere general acceptance of such a principle would mark an incalculable advance in the relations between higher and lower races. The expression of it is perhaps the most adventurous piece of idealism in the Covenant. Yet it is certainly not unpractical. It fits in with the practice of the best Governors of British Crown Colonies and Dependencies. Good instances may be found in the administration of Nigeria and Tanganyika by Great Britain, of Samoa by New Zealand, and I may be allowed to add, of Papua by Australia. But it is much in advance of the beliefs or the practice of most of the self-governing colonies of the British Empire, not to speak of the tropical possessions of some other Powers. The white man ruling in a black man's country has normally an attitude on this question utterly different from that accepted by educated opinion at home. Consequently, the framers of the League machinery have taken great trouble to secure that the principles of Article XXII are carried out. A special Mandate is drawn up for each Territory; it is commented on by the Mandates Commission and approved by the Council. Then each Mandatory Power has to send in to the Mandates Commission an annual report on the administration of its territory, and to send a representative to answer questions and supply such additional information as the Commission may require.

The Commission is a highly competent body, consisting mainly of ex-administrators of special reputation and experience. But anyone can see that it has before it an arduous and slippery task in which it deserves the intelligent and unstinted support of every man and woman who values good government and hates cruelty. If it ventures on any strong criticism, it usually has against it the Government of the Mandatory State, the local officials criticized, and in most self-governing colonies, the local public opinion. It has against it all the selfish interests of Governments and dominant classes; and for it nothing but the possible sympathies of such of the "natives" as know of its existence and hear anything of its actions, and the conscience of a small part of civilized mankind. That conscience, when it can be awakened, speaks clearly enough; but it is hard to rouse, except by undesirable stunts and scandals, and it is seldom active outside a small ring of advanced nations, normally led by Great Britain. The Mandates Commission may do its work with the utmost tact and care, but it can hardly succeed unless it has the unfaltering and intelligent support of the Great Powers. Unfortunately this has not always been forthcoming.

The detailed Minutes of the Permanent Mandates Commission make poignant and varied reading. At times one can watch the meeting of present administrators, whose problems are actually before them, with famous old administrators, who faced and solved similar problems long ago. Each side helps the other; and you feel that, amid all its difficulties, the "sacred trust" is being well carried out. At times one is conscious of suppressions in the report of the Mandatory, of unexplained contradictions between that report and the evidence that comes from other sources; one catches a dim vision of sufferings concealed and petitions for justice suppressed, and the Commission baffled in its efforts to discover the truth. The Commission has no power to visit a Mandated Territory, nor to send an inspector, nor yet to confront the representative of the Mandatory with witnesses who have told a different story. Any such testing of the facts must rest with the Council, and the Council has never yet been so impolite as to express in public a doubt of the perfect rectitude of all the agents of all its members. To do it justice, I hardly see how it could. What it could do, and possibly on occasion has done, is privately to let a Mandatory Power feel that some inquiry or change would "prevent misunderstandings". On the whole, however, the impression made is encouraging. Public opinion is a very subtle weapon, which pierces the joints of the harness of the most hardened bodies. A sentence in the Report of the Mandates Commission to the Council mentioning that the Commission is not quite satisfied as to this, or would like further information as to that, has a greater effect than anyone without experience could imagine.

Nor shall I ever forget a scene in the Assembly during the time when Sir Edgar Walton was senior delegate for South Africa. The negro delegate from Hayti, M. Bellegarde, stood up to demand in courteous and measured terms an immediate committee of inquiry into the action of the South African Government in suppressing the unrest among the Bondelswarts. It was one coloured man challenging not only South Africa but the whole British Empire, because of a wrong, a grave wrong, done to a tiny tribe of impoverished Hottentots. I admired M. Bellegarde for his courage. And I must say I was proud of the way in which all the British Delegations, from South Africa onwards, immediately, without any resentment, agreed to the fullest inquiry. Had anything like that ever been seen in the world before? The Mandates Commission has once or twice been "let down" by the League Council. But in the main the Mandate system has proved itself an unqualified success. If the League lives and grows, the Mandate system ought gradually to be extended to all the tropical territories of the civilized Powers. A beginning might well be made in the "unification" of Uganda and Kenya with the mandated area of Tanganyika, as suggested in the East Africa Blue Book (1929).

In sum it seems to me that the Covenant, though not without certain ambiguities and loopholes, is on the whole a wonderfully successful instrument, flexible, comprehensive, and exactly directed to the main evil which it was desired to cure. It does aim straight at the heart of the international anarchy; and it does so by a method which is calculated to stir up the very minimum of opposition. Its normal sanction is the public opinion of the world; its most effective weapon publicity. You cannot punish a nation; you cannot even coerce by force any moderately strong nation. But you can exert a very severe pressure on even the strongest to mend its ways by simply putting a question to its representative at the Assembly, or at one of the permanent Commissions, and publishing its reply.

Personally I am in favour of "filling the gaps in the Covenant" and making some of the engagements more definite. Yet if the Council of the League, under its present leaders, were really using its powers under the Covenant for all they are worth, there would be little need to fill gaps. If they even were willing to work whole-heartedly at the things that involve no risk of war, one could forgive them for not accepting in the meantime any obligations concerning that extreme hazard. They would at least be fostering the spirit of peace and international trust. The trouble is that they do not always work whole-heartedly. The world has changed, and they have not changed with it. Of course, no one wants war; the Great Powers are sincerely anxious to keep on good terms with one another. But one feels that the great constructive undertakings of the League and the International Labour Organization, Disarmament, Arbitration, the Suppression of the Dangerous Drugs Traffic and the White Slave Traffic, Mandates, Protection of Minorities, the International Eight-Hours Day and the recommendations of the Economic Conference, are too often approached by the representatives of the Great Powers with a curious inertia, if not with active dislike. There would be trouble in Europe if they actively opposed the work of the League; but they can, and do, abstain from actively helping it. No doubt a fairly powerful section in the Governments, in the Press and in the party organizations, dislikes the League for itself and dislikes it the more for the causes it undertakes. Their names recall the kind of causes that have been advocated at home by "intellectuals" and "faddists", and "humanitarians" and "tiresome women", and all the classes which the sound Philistine party-politician most distrusts. Consequently, since open opposition is not safe, such people try to reduce the League's sphere of action. They cripple it by attacks on the budget. They suppress the reports

INSIDE THE COVENANT

of committees so that public opinion may not operate. They explain that the League is an infant which must not be entrusted with serious work until it has grown stronger, and meantime they take due steps to prevent its growing.. The ideal of these critics would probably be to keep the regular meetings of the Council, with the Great Powers as an inner ring, while gradually reducing to vanishing point the rest of the League's activities.

There is danger here. For it must be recognized by all moderate men that in the Governments of the first and second rank of nations since the war reactionary and conservative influences have been extremely strong, progressive and liberal influences exceptionally weak. The reasons for this state of things are fairly clear: the overwhelming general determination to have no dealings with revolution, and the incessant and discreditable feuds of the progressive parties among themselves. But the effect on the fortunes of the League has been discouraging, and has been made worse by the habit, adopted by the party Governments in some countries, such as Italy, Spain, and (since 1925) Great Britain, of sending to the Assembly purely party delegations, instead of mixed delegations representative of the nation as a whole, as is the practice of France, Germany, and Belgium.

No doubt the greater part of the League's work makes a severe demand on the average party politician. It requires him to study new problems, and problems in which his electorate has no direct personal interest. It demands that he shall face fresh problems with fresh thought, discard obsolete conceptions, and see steadily beyond the limits of the old "sovereign independent state". The whole enterprise of the League is a great adventure, and an adventure based upon a great Repentance. It needs, both in the nations themselves and in the men who serve the nations, a high level of mental activity, a determination to fulfil obligations and to do equal justice to the strong and the weak. In this requirement there has certainly been much failure. The presence or absence, on Council or Commission, of one strong and sincere man with a gift of leading makes far more difference than it should. And I fear that many of those who have watched international policies closely for the last ten years come away with the same impression: that the average present-day Government does not yet realize how small and transient are the gains, how large and enduring the losses, that result from small failures in moral courage and the lack of complete honesty. It is a lesson which good business firms had learnt generations ago.

V

THE WORLD OUTSIDE THE COVENANT AND ITS DANGERS

ONE does not expect the League system to deal with all human ills; but there are several subjects, not obviously unsuitable for mention in the Covenant, which were, as a matter of fact, left out. The first that occurs to the mind is Civil War. It occurs the more obviously because of late years there has been so much of it. Morocco, Syria, China, are ill-omened names; though it is surely rather a significant fact that the kind of war which the League was meant to stop has been stopped, the kind which the League could not touch has continued. The League is a purely international body; it is there to prevent the outbreak of wars between nations, but it has, of course, no right to intervene in any of its members' internal affairs. Each member of the League has its own constitution, monarchy, republic, dictatorship or what you will, its own way of forming a government and of choosing its delegates. The League merely looks to the credentials of the delegates and sees that they are signed by the proper authority. During the civil war in China, for example, while the Government of Peking was supreme it sent its delegates to the League; when the issue of the war was doubtful the Peking delegate continued to exist but remained prudently inactive while an unofficial envoy from the South came and kept watch upon him; when the Southern forces were victorious, a new delegation was sent from Nanking. It may seem a spiritless policy for the League to sit impotently by while one of its members is distracted by civil war, but a little reflection will convince most people that interference would be worse. The Holy Alliance had a definite principle; it supported legitimacy, and was ready to suppress all rebellion. The Soviet Government, in so far at least as it is represented by the Communist International, has the contrary principle: in opposition to a capitalist world it supports all rebellion. But to the League one principle is as impossible as the other. The League leaves the domestic troubles of its member-nations entirely alone.

An exception must be made for a civil war which is leading, or likely to lead, to international war. Any such "threat of war" can be raised under Article XI and the Council is then free to take "any action that may be deemed wise and effectual to safeguard the peace". Foreign intervention in the domestic quarrels of any nation is always a most dangerous expedient; but the mere fact of being engaged in civil war does not confer a special inviolability on a nation which is threatening the peace of its neighbours.

There is one other situation in which war is not forbidden under the Covenant. When two nations have brought their dispute before the Council and, after due consideration, the Council cannot agree on its recommendation, the two parties recover their freedom of action. Obviously, disputes which would divide the Council may well occur; and great efforts have been made to prohibit this kind of war also. Now there is no nation more completely innocent than Great Britain of any design to plot against its neighbours; there is no nation to whom continuous peace is so vital a necessity. Yet ever since 1924 the debates of the League have been largely occupied in a prolonged struggle by Great Britain against most of the rest of Europe, in order to keep alive the "right of war" and to prevent the extension of arbitration. This has generally been represented at home as a refusal to undertake wider responsibilities in preventing war abroad, but the pretext is a little thin. For although the supporters of the Geneva Protocol advocated both the complete prohibition of war and also the enforcement of that prohibition by economic and military action, the Scandinavians and Poles more than once proposed a simple treaty for the complete abolition of war with no extension of sanctions, and the British delegation remained no less obdurate. Great Britain would never agree to abstain from all war. She would never accept any obligation to arbitrate all disputes, nor even all disputes of a legal character.

By a curious stroke of fortune, the objectionable proposal which had been so steadily refused suddenly reappeared from a quarter which no European Government liked to meet with a negative.

The United States, which had hitherto kept almost ostentatiously aloof from the general peace movement of the world, was led, in the course of negotiations for a special treaty with France, to propose a universal treaty for the complete "renunciation of war as an instrument of national policy".

It was an immense gain to get the United States once more interested in the peace movement; it removed one of the great dangers confronting the League to have the United States practically committed, as it would be committed by this treaty, to refrain from supporting a treaty-breaking and peace-breaking state against the boycott or blockade of the League. And, as we have said, an absolute prohibition of war was just what most of the states of Europe—all, indeed, except Italy and Great Britain—had been clamouring for. Nevertheless, the course of negotiations proved to be not quite simple.

There were, first of all, two obvious questions to be asked: Did this absolute renunciation of war forbid united action to coerce an "aggressor" as laid down by the Covenant or the Treaty of Locarno? And did it forbid wars of self-defence? The first point was simple: the "aggressor" would by hypothesis already have broken his treaty, and obviously no Power can at the same time break a treaty and claim the protection of that treaty. The new treaty did not, indeed, expressly provide any sanctions against a Power which should break it, but it certainly did not forbid them. And to renounce war as "an instrument of national policy" was not to forbid it as a means of agreed international policy. The Covenant and the other League treaties were in no way contrary to the proposed pact.

As to the second point the discussion took a curious turn. European nations were accustomed to the distinction between "aggressive" and "defensive" war, and, realizing that this real difference was in practice liable to confusion and misrepresentation, they had worked hard, and on the whole successfully, both in the Protocol and the Treaty of Locarno, to establish a satisfactory and clearly ascertainable test of "aggression". American opinion, on the other hand, not having followed these discussions and being constitutionally contemptuous of subtleties, treated the difference between "aggressive" and "defensive" wars as so much hair-splitting. No nation ever admitted that it was making an aggressive war; all war must be renounced, and renounced absolutely.

The facts avenged themselves, as they so often do when ignored. When questioned by the French about "defensive" and "aggressive" wars, Mr. Kellogg explained that his treaty did renounce war without qualification, but that no treaty could ever do away with the sacred and inalienable right of self-defence. So far, so good. The American and European phraseology was different, the meaning was exactly the same. But then Mr. Kellogg in his championship of the right of self-defence went far further than European opinion, as expressed in the Covenant, at all approved. He stated in so many words that each nation must be judge in its own case: "It alone is competent to decide whether circumstances require recourse to war in self-defence".[1] This admission obviously knocks an extremely large hole in the treaty. For any nation which is not bound by the Covenant it practically restores the old freedom to make war when it chooses. The Covenant, of course, insists that, before making war, a member of the League must submit his dispute to the Council or Assembly, and fortunately the new treaty, though it does not take away any right of self-defence which its signatories may possess, certainly does not confer any new one. It does not in any way repeal or supersede the Covenant.

Thus, the questions raised between America and the chief European Powers were promptly, if not satisfactorily, settled. They had always wished for the prohibition of war, but there remained Great Britain who did not. Diplomatic considerations and the pressure of public enthusiasm at home and in most of the Dominions made it impossible to reject the Kellogg proposal, yet the Government's objection to an absolute renunciation of war remained unshaken. The delay of the British Government in answering was unexpectedly long. The letter of acceptance was elaborate and cautious, and

[1] Note of the Government of the United States, June 3, 1928.

contained one stipulation of a very peculiar character:—

> There are certain regions of the world the welfare and integrity of which constitutes a special and vital interest for our peace and safety. H.M.G. have been at pains to make it clear in the past that interference with these regions cannot be suffered. Their protection against attack is to the British Empire a measure of self-defence. It must be clearly understood that H.M.G. in Great Britain accept the new treaty on the distinct understanding that it does not prejudice their freedom of action in this respect. (May 19, 1928.)

"So that was the explanation", said European diplomatists; "at last they have stated it!" Great Britain is reluctant to sign universal treaties, or accept obligatory arbitration, or curtail her "right of war", because she is an Empire, and an Empire is a thing with one foot inside civilization and one outside, in part resting on freedom, law, and representative government, and in part on conquest and force. In her relations to Europe and America and her own Dominions, Great Britain represents the peaceful and law-abiding League spirit as well as any community in Christendom, but as a ruling Power in Asia and Africa she belongs to a world in a different stage of civilization and speaking a different language. The general contention is perfectly true. There *are* "regions of the world" in which Great Britain might, at any moment, be compelled to act suddenly, violently, without waiting either for the establishment of external aggression or the authority of a judicial decision. When a hostile

Pathan tribe makes a raid upon a friendly tribe on the Indian frontier and escapes with its booty, no League procedure is really applicable. You cannot summon the tribe before the Council or ask it to lay its case before the International Court. The only thing is to attack and pursue the robbers with the nearest military force available. When Arabs from the desert come plundering into Iraq, when Russian agents stir up a seditious outbreak in India or the Far East, such actions do not really belong to the League world; they belong to something more primitive. And, of course, it is true that the sign of serious danger may be something far short of actual warfare.

It is supposed to have been anxiety about Egypt, half in, half outside, the Empire, that chiefly moved His Majesty's Government. However the statement was not well received. No other nation supported it. And the United States, while carefully answering the points raised by the other nations, made no reference whatever to this. The silence was the more marked because the British Note, somewhat indiscreetly, tried by a reference to the Monroe Doctrine to suggest that the United States really claimed and exercised the same liberty. This allusion has given some offence, because in American opinion the Monroe Doctrine is not an assertion of imperialist claims but a principle of liberation, protecting the independence of the South American republics.[1]

---

[1] The famous "doctrine" was stated in President Monroe's message to Congress on December 2, 1823, after the overthrow of

To me the stipulation seems on the one hand to mean something reasonable, and on the other to be stated in far too sweeping terms. The "regions" in which a free right of war is claimed are not defined or described. The right of saying whether any particular country is one of them rests with His Majesty's Government, who will mention it when the time suits. In the second place the thing that "cannot be suffered" is

Spanish and Portuguese rule in America: "We owe it to candour and to the amicable relations existing between the United States and those Powers to declare that we should consider any attempt on their part to extend their system to any portion of this hemisphere as dangerous to our peace and safety. With the existing colonies or dependencies of any European Power we have not interfered and shall not interfere. But with the [South American] Governments who have declared their independence and maintained it, and whose independence we have on great consideration and on just principles acknowledged, we could not view any interposition for the purpose of oppressing them, or controlling in any other manner their destiny, by any European Power in any other light than as the manifestation of an unfriendly disposition towards the United States." Since that time President Wilson (December 7, 1915) deliberately substituted for the conception of guardianship and wardship the other conception of partnership "upon a footing of equality and genuine independence".

Compare Mr. Elihu Root's address to the American Society of International Law in 1916: "The message of Monroe affirmed in effect that all the American states were to be regarded as members of the community of nations; that they were entitled to live, to be independent, to be treated as equals, and to be free from oppression by other Powers." This speech of Mr. Root's was mentioned with approval in 1923 by Mr. Secretary Hughes, who added, after quoting the words of Chief Justice Marshall: "No principle of general law is more universally acknowledged than the perfect equality of nations. ... We have not sought by opposing the intervention of Non-American Powers to establish a protectorate or overlordship of our own with respect to these republics. Such a pretension is not only not found in the Monroe Doctrine, but would be in opposition to our fundamental affirmative policy." (1923.) He took the same line at the Pan-American Congress at Havana in 1928.

"interference". A later sentence also speaks of "attack", which is clear; but "interference" might mean anything. It might mean successful commercial or cultural penetration; it might mean the establishment of a factory, or a school, or a native university with foreign teachers, or anything to which Great Britain objected. The pledge thus becomes: "I solemnly renounce war as an instrument of national policy, unless anything happens which I do not like in certain parts of the world which happen to interest me." Literally taken, this interpretation destroys the force of the new pact as completely as Mr. Kellogg's claim about self-defence. One can only be thankful, once again, that the gaps in the new treaty have no power to create similar gaps in the Covenant. Thanks to the Covenant, there are still no regions of the world, outside the British Empire itself, in which Great Britain has the right to make war on her own impulse and for her own purposes without first seeking peaceful settlement; just as there are no circumstances in which any League member can simply declare war without reference to the League on the ground that she considers the war defensive. Articles XII–XVII forbid.

As far as I can see, there is only one special "reservation" or "explanation" on grounds of Empire, which Great Britain ought to make before accepting the whole system of peaceful settlement implied in the Covenant and the Court Statute. When the time comes, as it surely must, for signing the Optional Clause of the Court Statute—i.e. for accepting the principle of Judicial Settlement for all international disputes of a legal character—she should make it clear that Great Britain regards disputes which may arise between different parts of the Empire as domestic and not international. This exclusion is justified both in theory and in practice. A dispute between, say, England and Australia, is clearly domestic to the British Commonwealth and ought to be decided in accordance with British ideas and British customs. To hand it over to the International Court, to be decided according to the Court's view of international law, would be to give to a semi-foreign tribunal the right of determining the constitution of the British Empire. In practice, moreover, there might be a real inconvenience in giving to some discontented or disruptive Government, such as has sometimes existed in Ireland and elsewhere, the right to raise problems on which continental law was expected to be different from British, and to compel other British Governments to appear before the Court.

A less justifiable objection to any acceptance of the Optional Clause is based, not on the unity of the Empire, but on its diversity. It is argued that the relations of Great Britain towards different parts of the Empire are extremely various: Canada and New Zealand have a different attitude from that of South Africa or Ireland; India from that of Kenya; British India from the Native States, and so on; and further, that the Empire itself shades off imperceptibly into something less than empire—a control of foreign relations, a right of advice, or merely an indefinite and not altogether welcome "interest". The constitution of the British Empire is unwritten and probably unwritable. How is it possible to apply to all parts of it a common formula or to sign a single multilateral treaty to which all of these different communities may or must adhere?

This argument seems to me more plausible than convincing. A man may have the most varied and indefinite relations to his wife, his brother, his bootmaker, his political opponent, his rival in love, or his defaulting debtor; but he is expected to act towards all of them conformably to the laws of his country. Everything goes wrong as soon as we make a distinction, in President Wilson's words, "between those to whom we wish to be just and those to whom we do not wish to be just". The broad principles of non-aggression and obedience to law, as laid down in the Covenant and the Court Statute, are surely elastic enough to be suitable to all cases, and if applied conscientiously would relieve the few remaining Imperial Powers of a huge dead-weight of suspicion and misrepresentation.

The whole difficulty comes, as suggested above, from the fact that empires have one foot in the civilized world and one in the uncivilized. In this respect Great Britain does not stand entirely alone. France, Holland, and Portugal all have some savage or imperfectly civilized subjects and neighbours. It is surely most unwise for Great Britain to court unpopularity and suspicion by claiming a sort of superiority to the law, all by herself. She might at least find out whether the others wish to make similar claims. Not that I believe there is need for any of them to claim, either in form or in reality, extra-legal privileges. Troubles with their own savage subjects are their own domestic concern. Those in their mandated areas are dealt with under the Mandate system. There remain only the troubles incident to any "savage frontier"—i.e. to the juxtaposition of wild people and civilized people. I have never heard of a wild tribe ingeniously remaining inside the provisions of a complicated treaty while provoking their civilized neighbours to a breach of it. All that seems to be needed is that, when some abnormal friction occurs, a report on the circumstances should be laid before the Council of the League at the earliest possible moment. This is the precedent set by Sir Austen Chamberlain with regard to British action both in China and in Egypt, in both cases with admirable results.

The truth is that empires, such as are left of them, are in a perilous position. The German, Austrian, and Russian Empires are fallen; China is in chaos; Japan much exhausted, and scarcely an empire; France has no independent Dominions and not much reserve of strength. The United States has but few foreign possessions and not many client republics. It formally renounced in

1915 all claim to control the policies of South America. Great Britain stands pre-eminent as representing in every part of the world a shaken and unpopular principle, the rule of human beings by an alien race. And Great Britain, too, is in retreat. The Dominions are independent; they sign their own treaties, and the name "Imperial Parliament" is no longer allowed.[1] Apart from slight restrictions in each case, Ireland has won her independence by force, India is actively seeking it, Iraq has been granted it. Even the white settlers in Kenya can successfully refuse to obey His Majesty's Government. And meantime the British good name is incessantly the prey of bitter and unscrupulous propaganda, reaching from Russia to China, from China to America and most of Europe, and backed, as perhaps no propaganda known to history has been before, by the resources and policy of one Great Power and by more or less organized groups in every land. The public opinion of the world counts to-day more than it has in the past. The disinterested approval or disapproval of the middle-sized states, and of the stable and civilized small states, is an important source of strength or of weakness. And for the first time in history the public opinion of the civilized world has now, through the League, an instrument for expressing itself. It seems to me that a lesson lies here for all the old empires, and for Great Britain most of all. If they try to claim special privileges, either that of having "free

[1] See further in Lecture VII, p. 211 f.

hands" when other nations are bound, or of secrecy where other nations are not secret, or of being in other unspecified ways above the law that binds the rest of the League, I think they will run a grave danger of uniting the public opinion of the civilized world against the whole principle of Empire. They lead the world at present; but for that very reason they are more exposed to criticism than smaller states; and a leadership based on mere force, unaccompanied by public respect, cannot under modern conditions endure for long. The real conduct of Great Britain is, in my opinion, more scrupulous and unaggressive than that of any other Great Power, and it seems to me a most exasperating form of folly for her, when acting like a virtuous policeman, to claim on paper the privileges of a pirate.

The principle of Empire—that is, the government of alien territories or nations by a superior or stronger nation—fits with some difficulty into the scheme of the Covenant. There is a place made for it in Article XXII. The Mandate system imposes on the Imperial Powers exactly the right degree and kind of control, but unfortunately it covers only a small part of the subject territories of the world. It shows, however, the right road, and a large part of the greatest problem of Great Britain's future will be on the way to solution as soon as some British Government takes the bold but eminently wise step of sending the annual reports of all its Crown Colonies and Protectorates to the League Mandates Commission, and thereby establishing the Mandate principle as the only true and accepted method for the government of the uncivilized peoples by the civilized.

But a large part of the human race is still outside the Covenant altogether. Most of the Moslem world, except Persia, is still outside; and the relations of the Moslem to the Christian civilization are greatly, and perhaps increasingly, in need of some pacifying influence. The Moslem thinks his religion, with its sobriety, its monotheism, and its absence of idols, obviously superior to Christianity with its drunkenness, its idolatry, and its tritheism sometimes verging into polytheism. He thinks his severe and primitive civilization obviously superior to the luxury and vices of the West. Yet he finds himself everywhere in a position of inferiority or actual subjection to the Christian. One hears of the thrill of enthusiasm which swept through the Mohammedan world at the news of the rising of the Young Turks in 1908, of the victory of Mustapha Kemal, of the occasional successes of Abdul Krim against the French. Even the defeat of Russia by Japan in 1911 came as a gospel of good news; a Christian and European Great Power could after all be defeated by one that was not European and not Christian. I remember that during the war it was reported that Moslem opinion in India was impervious to any published statements; statements might always be, and mostly were, lies. Indian Moslems would only be influenced by photographs. But when genuine photographs were obtained of Jemal Pasha and his staff drinking champagne, they had to be thrown away. Against the Turkish leaders not even a photograph could be believed. How far this sentiment has been annulled by the anti-religious attitude of Mustapha Kemal one cannot say. Islam is after all a civilization rather than merely a religion. But it is certainly made stronger and more dangerous by the spread of Islam in Africa. I see that the Communist International has just acknowledged the Pan-African Revolutionary Movement and called upon all native Africans to rise against their white masters. But I doubt if Karl Marx and atheism will provide the necessary inspiration.

From the so-called "white-man's point of view" in its crudest form it would be best that the African should have no religion at all. Next best, that he should keep his own feeble and witch-ridden paganism. What the white nigger-driver instinctively dreads is a religion which shall teach the black labourer that he has an immortal soul as precious as that of the white man in the eyes of God. Such a religion "puts ideas" into the mind of the black; it makes him imagine that an act which would be a crime if committed against a white man is equally impermissible against himself; it makes him want to work for himself and not for a master. Now it seems certain that one or other of the great religions is bound to spread through Africa, either Islam or Christianity. And Islam, the more explosive of the two, is almost certain to win, both because it is in most ways nearer to the African level, because it does not interfere with polygamy, and because it will be to the negro something that is his own and free, not a thing imposed on him by his white masters.

I leave out of account the possible effects of the French policy of arming and training great negro armies, though it is worth remembering that Chaka, who created the Zulu Empire and deluged South Africa in blood, learnt the art of war as servant to a British soldier. It seems to me quite clear that so vast a mass of more or less united human feeling as Moslem Africa will soon present cannot possibly be held down by mere force. Doubtless the negro will not for a very long time to come be the equal of the white man; but that is no reason why he should not be treated with fairness and his "welfare and progress" regarded as a sacred trust. It is a race between the spirit of mere exploitation, still extant in South Africa and Kenya, and the spirit of duty, normal in most British governors and openly expressed in the Covenant. If the first prevails, I see no prospect except a series of massacres and internal wars. If the second, it will show that the spirit of the Covenant has a power of saving society even where the Covenant itself does not hold.

But there are other great regions outside the Covenant. Of America it is almost impossible to prophesy. The most uncompromising expressions of the peace spirit come from America; the most munificent charity, the most carefully thought-out schemes of consolation to suffering human beings, of help to education and religion. There has never in the history of the world been anything to equal the practical beneficence of American foundations and private societies and individuals to the rest of the world. But this splendid work is, after all, almost entirely the work of a small number of persons, a hundred thousand or so perhaps, out of a hundred million. Political action and the immediate issues of war and peace depend on the will, or perhaps the caprice, of the hundred million; and it does sometimes seem, to judge from newspapers and public speeches, as if the mass of the American public had been less sobered and educated by the late war, had remained more violent in imagination and action, and more self-satisfied in their nationalism than the nations of Western Europe. A comparison of the speeches made on Armistice Day, 1928, by Mr. Baldwin and Mr. Coolidge respectively, reveals not so much any great divergences in policy, but an extraordinary difference in spiritual experience. One sometimes feels towards the American public as the small Balkan nations are said to feel towards the English. No doubt they are very rich and strong and full of good-natured impulses; but they care for nobody, nobody can tell what they may want to do next, and as they turn to the right or the left their whim may spread prosperity or ruin. America is probably the one nation in the world which does not realize what war is and which could afford the luxury of another. I have seen more books and speeches by Americans speaking of "inevitable wars", and the need to "make oneself respected" by immense armaments, than by the nationals of any other country. Still, the work of national education by means of the universities, colleges, and churches is peculiarly vigorous in America, and the spirit of self-criticism in the educated classes peculiarly healthy and strong. And, after all, since no other nation can possibly attack America, and she has just inaugurated a treaty pledging herself never to resort to war except in self-defence, the danger of American aggression is perhaps remote.

The case of Russia is entirely different. Russia is not only outside the Covenant, and to a great extent outside the comity of non-communist Europe, but is confessedly an enemy of the Covenant and out to destroy the League. The position, like many bad positions, is logical enough. The League is the great instrument invented by modern man for preserving and improving the social order without either war or revolution. And the Bolsheviks believe that the social order is evil, cannot be improved, and ought to be destroyed everywhere by civil war. It must be remembered that the old order in Russia was infamously bad, not at all like the contemporary systems in France or England. The Government was habitually at war with its people, or at any rate with the best of its people. It encouraged drunkenness, it dreaded education, it lived by a murderous system of secret police, and it rewarded their crimes. Russia was at the end of the war a nation mad with suffering. The losses in the war were such as to make those of the British, or even the French, seem a trifle: 2,700,000 dead; 2,500,000 missing; total loss over five million as against our less than one. And the misery was aggravated by the knowledge of treachery in high places, by famine and by civil war. It is no wonder that, seeing the root of all their miseries in the old system, and identifying that system—quite wrongly—with what they call "Capitalism", the Russian Communists see in Western civilization a sort of upas-tree poisoning all beneath its shade.

The Communists are said by Trotsky to number at their best some 300,000 in a population of 120,000,000—say one Communist to four hundred ordinary folk. But they have dominated the nation. They represent, on the one hand, a new federal organization re-mapping the old centralized empire on the basis of nationality—a fine experiment if it can be honestly carried out; on the other hand, they form a new missionary religion at war with Western civilization. It is a religion like that of the French Revolution of 1789, but more militant and implacable. It has the dogmatism of a religion in its insistence on rewriting all history, all science and art, and—it is said—even mathematics, from the "proletarian" standpoint, in its persecution of free-thought and of any special individuality of character, in its weapon of "mass terror", its religious persecutions. And the disputes between the Second and the Third International have all the depth and venom of religious wars.

How is such a danger to be met? War can do nothing but harm. No foreign Power can conquer Russia, and every attack by a foreign Power will tend to unite the whole Russian people under its existing rulers. It is ultimately a struggle for life between two special systems and two religions: and that one will certainly win which is found to suit people best. Each system has its secret garrisons in the heart of the enemy's country. The Bolsheviks have their nests or "cells" among us, wherever throughout all Europe and America there are exceptionally impoverished or brutalized populations and exceptionally embittered hearts. The system of private property has its supporters in Russia, individually weak but in the mass innumerable, in the cottage of every peasant who wants to own his own farm. It seems to me clear that Communism in Russia cannot be permanent: Russia, if not a nation of serfs, must in the long run be a nation of peasant proprietors. If the Western nations can solve their economic troubles, maintain the peace, and progressively remove the worst discontents in their people, the Western system is bound to win.

Communism has already made its attack and has so far failed in most countries: in Hungary, Bulgaria, Germany, Great Britain, and even China, though we must not forget that three million people voted Communist in Germany at the last election. In a strife like this police measures are, of course, always necessary; but the issue will be decided, not by violent repression, and still less by wild language, but by the results of the two systems. If the Soviet system eventually produces a more satisfactory condition for its hundred and sixty million subjects than can be found elsewhere, Communism will spread. If the nations of Europe, by means of the League and the I.L.O., can not only get rid of the fear of war but remove their worst economic confusions and build up within their borders some approach to that "good life for man" which is the aim of civilization, Communism will decay and disappear. Meantime the problem, like our other problems, can only be solved by acting in the spirit of the Covenant even where the Covenant does not reach. This sort of strife is ultimately decided by third parties; and, when the forces are approximately equal, third parties will take the side of that system which seems to make people happy and that combatant who puts himself least in the wrong.

To turn to a different class of subject, Article XXIII of the Covenant makes provision "to secure and maintain . . . equitable treatment for the commerce of all members of the League". The clause means little enough, yet we are told that it was the only clause in Article XXIII that aroused much discussion. The bad shopkeeper thinks to prosper by damaging his neighbour's trade; and most nations are bad shopkeepers. Certainly this desire has been allowed to run riot in postwar Europe, producing its due consequences of poverty and ill will.

When the Allies were recognizing the independence of the successor states of the old Austrian Empire, they imposed various preliminary conditions, and it was hoped that one condition might be the maintenance of a customs union which would preserve freedom of trade throughout the whole territory that had once constituted the Austro-Hungarian Empire. Had that been done, Europe would have been saved from much of its long-continued economic distress. But the privilege which the new nations seemed to value next to the building up of armaments was that of erecting tariff walls against their neighbours and rivals. The game of beggar-my-neighbour set merrily in, combined with that of beggar-myself. In 1921, when most currencies were in a state of crisis and several nations on the verge of bankruptcy, the League called together at Brussels a great International Conference of expert financiers. The Conference unanimously recommended a number of economies, especially the balancing of budgets and the reduction of armaments, which the Governments at first ignored and then gradually and reluctantly put into partial practice, with the result that whereas in 1921 hardly any states had stable currencies, in 1927 they all had. Again, in 1925, owing to the

OUTSIDE THE COVENANT 159

prolonged economic distress of Europe, the Assembly asked the Council to convoke a most remarkable Conference of expert economists. The Conference, after much preparatory work, met in 1927: a hundred and ninety-four economists chosen by the Governments of fifty different nations, including the United States, Russia, and Turkey. It was the greatest and most authoritative conference ever summoned by the League; it seemed almost impossible that so vast a body of experts, taken from the nations with the most diverse traditions, should agree; yet the case was so clear that they did agree. The Report stated that in the world as a whole "production and consumption were greater than before the war". The trouble was that "there was no corresponding increase of international commerce". "Each nation's commerce is to-day being hampered by barriers established by other nations, resulting in a situation, especially in Europe, that is highly detrimental to the general welfare." The Conference unanimously recommends that "states should forthwith take steps to remove or diminish the tariff barriers that greatly hamper trade, starting with those that have been imposed to counteract the effect of disturbances arising out of the war". "The time has come to put an end to the increase of tariffs and to move in the opposite direction."

It seems almost impossible that all Governments should continue permanently to defy the unanimous advice of the economists whom they themselves appointed. It is tragic that Great Britain, who won her world pre-eminence by Free Trade, should choose the moment when even the most protectionist countries are repenting of their excesses to lead the movement back to high tariffs and restriction of commerce. The most innocent of all the offenders is again blocking the way to peace. One can only hope that, as happened with the Brussels Conference, in spite of the great difficulty of the first step, truth will have its effect in the long run.

Probably in the material world this question of the liberation of international trade is the most vital that confronts Europe. Tariffs never stand still. They will decrease or increase. An increase of protection in Europe and the British Dominions means not only the checking of commerce and the limitation of markets, the increased predominance of America with her market of 100,000,000 and of Russia with her market of 120,000,000 as against the miserable little national markets of the separate European states, or of Great Britain without its empire. It means also the wrecking of international co-operation and mutual help and the substitution of continual rivalry and hostile intrigue. It means the placing of a drawback on honest dealing and a premium on corruption, increased difficulties in the way of peace, and a long step in the direction of war. Free Trade is no doubt impossible in Europe for the time being; but there is no more momentous issue before the present generation than the question whether the

OUTSIDE THE COVENANT

world of commerce is to be organized on the basis of common advantage or in groups devoted to mutual injury.[1]

The Italian Government has more than once raised the important question concerning the distribution of raw materials. In the war, of course, they were controlled and rationed. Obviously, none of the Allies could be left destitute of the coal, iron, oil, or rubber that might be needed for carrying on the war. It may be long before there is a general recognition of a hardly less obvious truth, that no nation can be deliberately starved of the raw materials necessary for its economic life without a breach of the spirit of the Covenant and a danger of war. There was a policy at one time vigorously advocated in Great Britain, of holding the door of our tropical territories shut and keeping the raw materials produced within the Empire entirely to ourselves as an instrument of economic supremacy and, if need be, coercion.

[1] As evidence that I have not exaggerated the dangerous results of economic rivalry, I quote from a speech of Sir Arthur Salter at the Economic Conference of the International Federation of League of Nations Societies at Prague, October 4, 1928: " . . . We have ahead of us a form of international competition that is distinctive but not less dangerous. We must foresee a period of intense competition stimulated by two novel and distinctive features: the increasing standardization of America and the forced expansion of German exports under the pressure of the reparations obligation. If this intense competition is to take place without any of the restraints which prevent individual competition from breaking out into robbery and revolution—that is, without the restraints of social customs and a legal Code—I am terrified of the consequences upon the economic policies of Governments and upon the peace of the world."

The moral objections to such a policy are obvious. It is not international co-operation; it is not the "equitable treatment of the commerce of the rest of the League". The practical objection is that Great Britain holds too large a portion of the world's surface to be able to practise with impunity such selfishness. While we left trade free, other nations did not resent the immense extent of our possessions. Each one, if it could not have the territory itself, would sooner that it fell to Great Britain than to any other Power. If, in the change that has come over us since the war, we begin to say that our territories are our own farmland on which no foreign trader must trespass, the rest of the world must, I think, in time unite against a Power so vast and so intolerably oppressive.

One Article which stood in the original draft of the Covenant was, after some amendments in the course of discussions, eventually dropped. It provided for the "free exercise", in all states members of the League, of any religion whose practice was not "inconsistent with public order or public morals". The ground for inserting such an Article was that religious persecution may sometimes be a cause of war; the objection urged against it by the Belgian, Portuguese, Italian, and French delegations was that it would be inconsistent with the constitution of certain countries and "might be used by political parties against Governments". Any real danger of war arising from religious persecution could be dealt with under Article XI. The Article in some amended form, as suggested by Lord Robert Cecil and President Wilson, might have passed, had not the Japanese delegation raised a still more far-reaching question of principle by proposing to substitute a clause declaring that "the equality of nations being a basic principle of the League of Nations, the High Contracting Parties agree to accord to all alien nationals of states members of the League equal and just treatment in every respect, making no distinction either in law or fact on the ground of race or nationality". The division of sentiment was curious, and almost the opposite of that on the question of religion. The French were bound by the principles of the Revolution to admit the general equality of mankind, while certain British delegations could not contemplate giving equal rights to coloured men. On the whole the questions involved were held to be so controversial that they were better postponed. "Equality" is always a dangerous word, since so very few things in the world are really equal and all sweeping proclamations about equality consequently untrue. But distinctions before the law are always objectionable; and it seems likely that, unless civilization suffers a relapse, such distinctions "on the ground of race, nationality, or religion" are bound to disappear.

Another Italian proposal dealt with the question of free migration. Italy at that time wanted room abroad for her over-prolific population, and her claim met with much sympathy. It was proposed that members of the League should freely admit one another's nationals, for visit or for residence, provided, of course, there was no ground of objection apart from nationality. America and the British Dominions, however, have for long been passionately opposed to such freedom of migration, and of late years Great Britain too, for the first time in her history, has become infected with the anti-alien complex. Ministers expatiate with pride on the large numbers of foreigners, guilty of no offence, who have been driven away from British ports in the course of a year. Economists will explain this policy as so much bad economics; psychologists, going a little deeper, will perhaps recognize in it the old well-known lust of persecution which is more or less chronic in the maltreatment of Japanese and Chinese in Australia and California, of negroes in the Southern States, or of Jews in Russia. It is all odious and, one would have thought, un-English.

On the other hand, it has to be admitted that the right of free migration would have dangerous consequences. Already in the United States there are places where the population is too heterogeneous to be satisfactory, either physically or politically. And what would America not give to be rid of the ten million negroes whose ancestors she imported in chains against their will? With free migration the most prolific races would spread far and wide over the earth; and the most prolific are certainly not the highest.

Look at a map of the Pacific Ocean. It is almost a British sea, as the Mediterranean is a Latin sea. It is almost surrounded by what are called Anglo-Saxon races or territories: Australia, New Zealand, the United States, Canada. Now the northern and north-western shores of the Pacific are about the most over-populated parts of the world. The crowding is immense, the birth-rate and death-rate terrific. I remember a Chinese delegate at the League of Nations expressing surprise at the emotion which Europeans showed at the million or so deaths from the Russian famine: "Many millions of our people died of famine a few years ago, and nobody minded."

On the southern and south-eastern shores there are great areas temperate and under-populated —all British Columbia, the Canadian coast, California and South America; also the empty and undeveloped plains of Australia, kept empty partly by climate, partly by deliberate legislation.

Are those populations which are dying for lack of land to be kept permanently excluded from these territories which are enfeebled by lack of population? The Australians and Americans say firmly, "Yes"; and there can be no doubt of their perfect right to say so, according to all principles of international law. They intend to keep their country a white-man's country and not to have it flooded by enormous masses of a recklessly prolific race, which has certainly a much lower standard of living and, according to Western notions, a lower standard of civilization. Is it on the whole for the good of the world that a large part of the earth's surface should be kept as a reserve for the white races, or rather predominantly for the Anglo-Saxons and those who mix well with them; or is the whole world to be overrun by whatever tribes of the *genus homo* breed quickest and take the lowest wages?

The first alternative seems possibly selfish or arrogant. Few thinking persons would like to see the world given over, like parts of America, to pure Anglo-Saxondom. But the second alternative is absolutely intolerable to contemplate. Populations which breed like flies to the limit of subsistence, and die like flies when the weather changes, can never build up a standard of life or character worthy of the dignity of man. The future of civilization surely lies with the nations of low birth-rate and still lower death-rate, whose members demand for themselves and their neighbours a good standard of health, strength, and conduct, room to move in, fair conditions to work in, and leisure in which to play, rest, and think.

The answer to our question is in principle clear, but the application of it raises some of the vastest problems affecting the future of mankind. There is still time to have them studied as they should be studied, patiently, dispassionately, in an international spirit, by the intellectual co-operation of those in different nations who are best qualified. But by the next generation time will press; by the next after that there may be no time at all.

VI

FROM CHAOS TO COSMOS: THE BUILDING OF A NEW ORDER AND THE NEED OF INTELLECTUAL CO-OPERATION

WE spoke in an earlier discussion of the alternations produced in human evolution between order and disorder, attainment and painful striving, Cosmos and Chaos. "*All things were together*", said Anaxagoras, "*till Thought came and arranged them.*" That process is being constantly repeated through history. Mankind strives to attain some satisfactory system of belief, of knowledge, of social organization, of daily habits. He attains it; and before long it fails in some detail to give satisfaction, or is upset by some new influence from outside. He finds, let us say, in the matter of belief the Catholic Church; in knowledge the Ptolemaic system of astronomy; in social organization the early Chinese Empire; in daily habits the law of the Jews or the fixed daily customs of the Moslems. If such a cosmos breaks down too soon, it is scarcely a cosmos, and has no influence; if it lasts too long, it is fatal to progress and collapses eventually in great disorder, as the history of China illustrates. Sooner or later man finds his ordered Cosmos fail him and he wanders once more out to

> . . . the waste beyond God's peace,
> To maddening freedom and bewildering light,

there to build afresh out of new materials the unattained Cosmos of his desire.

We suggested above that the age of Nineteenth-Century Liberalism was, comparatively speaking, a Cosmos. Not merely a great age, or an age in which society seemed on the whole successful, but an age possessing a definite form and character, in which people knew what to expect of the world and how to live in it.

The test of a Cosmos, apart from the general contentment which it produces, both moral and intellectual, is that the range of effective discussion or strife is limited and the extremes not unreconcilable. Now I think it will be admitted, if we take the foundations of society as being the family, the state, and something which for the moment we may call religion or fundamental belief, the Victorian Age in England did on the whole maintain towards these three ultimates a position fairly concordant with itself, or at least not torn by irreconcilable discords. With regard to marriage and the family, for instance, though all later Victorian literature is incessantly criticizing the institution and demanding reforms, there was in Great Britain a large basis of common agreement. In France or Italy, no doubt, it was easy to find Catholics who regarded marriage as indissoluble and divorce and remarriage as punishable with the pains of hell; while close beside them you would find the champions of mere promiscuity. Both views were eminently un-Victorian. The Victorian was in favour of greater freedom in the marriage laws, much greater freedom in the education of children and the general relation of children to parents; he regularly derided feminine jealousy and masculine authoritarianism. But all parties alike believed generally in the duty of children to parents, parents to children, and married people to one another, and thought it an obvious disaster and disgrace if family affection markedly failed.

With regard to the state, there were no conspirators, neither to restore the Stuarts nor to overthrow the monarchy. Everyone accepted the principle of representative government; everyone accepted the constitution and everyone wished to improve it by some changes. No one advocated the use of violence or fraud in order to make the will of a minority prevail over that of the nation. There was a general agreement to praise freedom: some wanted much more of it and some only a little, but all were in favour of it, and scarcely any recommended attaining it by breaking the law. They believed in Parliament, and in all its implications: the value of free speech, the right of a minority to have a fair hearing for its unpopular views, the duty of representatives to deal honestly by their constituents, and the duty of all to submit when fairly outvoted. Along with these beliefs went a profound respect for political leaders, and a general expectation that they should be men of high personal character. A latent conflict between the ideas of Empire abroad and Democratic Freedom at home was reconciled by the rather optimistic but by no means hypocritical theory that British rule was educating its subject peoples to be free.

It may be paradoxical to suggest that in a time so conspicuous for free-thought, and even for scepticism, a time when an observant English clergyman could attend the services of over a hundred different religious bodies in London alone, there was any general agreement on religion. Yet I believe, in the truest sense of that slippery word, there was. If, looking beneath the dogmatic creeds which people fight about and the conflicting sects to which they belong, we try to consider the sort of fundamental belief on which they seriously act, the sort of faith by which they really live and for which they would, if necessary, incur danger and sacrifice, I think there was a large degree of concord at the heart of the Victorian Age. Take a Broad Churchman, a strict Nonconformist, a Secularist preacher, an enlightened Conservative M.P. with no great interest in religion, and put to them some of the fundamental issues which would have roused violent dissensions in other periods of history: ought the poor to be educated, ought Jews or heretics to be persecuted, is a hell of eternal torment consistent with the goodness of God, is a man bound to live for others as well as for himself, is there some purpose or some good end towards which man is striving and by which the suffering of life is in some sense and to some degree justified?—there would be a consensus of opinion in the Nineteenth-Century England far greater than at any other time. There was a real and enthusiastic escape from the dominion of unproved dogma; an acceptance of the results of science, provided, of course, they are duly guaranteed by the authorities; and a no less firm acceptance of what are loosely called "Christian morals", i.e. the lines of conduct approved by the general experience of the Christian nations and developed by two thousand years of human progress. The divergences were matters for discussion, not mortal oppositions. The general agreement prevailed over the occasional difference.

I do not wish to labour the point, but I think most people will agree that this Cosmos has largely broken down. We find at the present day among the educated classes a larger amount of violent oppositions, a much smaller one of steady general concord. In religion we have a reaction towards Roman Catholicism and imitations thereof; a great output of new and more or less fantastic superstitions drawn indifferently from the mysterious East or the neurotic West; also a large and outspoken rejection of all religion and particularly of all morality. These oppositions cannot easily be resolved or reduced to agreement. They involve extremes of reaction, religious, military, and political, together with extreme licence and rebellion.

There is an increase of pacifism together with an increase of militarism. We have the Pact of Paris for the Renunciation of War and public services and rejoicings to celebrate it. We have a Conservative Prime Minister saying that one more war in the West will be the end of civilization. Yet nationalism, the stupidest and most dangerous of public vices, ramps and rages, not only in countries like China, where it was provoked by long oppression, but in America and even Scotland, which are commonly supposed to rule the world.[1] If you ask foreign observers what change they chiefly notice in England as compared with the time before the war, nine out of ten of them will say: The increase of soldiers, of recruiting advertisements, of military pageants,

---

[1] Where, for example, in modern history could one find a parallel to the following decree, permitting *certain classes* of foreigners to reside *temporarily* in Rumania? And probably Rumania is not the worst offender in this respect!

A decree concerning the extension of permits authorizing foreigners to reside in Rumania came into force on October 8th. The main provisions of the decree are as follows:—

"(1) Extensions for three years will be granted to:—

"Foreigners born in Rumania and resident permanently in the country, with the exception of those born in the annexed provinces who opted for another nationality.

"Foreigners who served in the Rumanian Army during the war.

"Foreigners of Rumanian origin."

It then explains that extensions for two years and for one year will be granted to certain very limited classes. Then: "Permits will not be extended for foreigners in the following categories:—

"Commercial clerical *personnel*, engineers and chemists, with special exceptions, or those who had been admitted by the Central Immigration Commission.

"Workmen in the petrol, mining, sugar, chocolate, and tobacco industries, and all manual workers in general, with the exception of skilled workers and foremen (not including drillers in the petrol industry).

"All foreigners who do not fall into the categories enumerated in the list of those whose permits may be extended." (*The Times*, October 16, 1928.)

of military organizations in schools, of constant talk about bombs, tanks, poison gases, and all the circumstances of war. Take all the leading Christian nations, Great Britain, France, Germany, and America: each one, though partially consoled by the consciousness of its own virtue, is profoundly disturbed by the militarism of all the rest. To take one slight but significant piece of evidence: there is in Gilbert and Sullivan's opera, *H.M.S. Pinafore*, a parody of a patriotic song; the original audiences, of course, saw it was a parody and laughed at it, but post-war audiences think it is a real patriotic song and applaud! I do not know if there is a greater clash than before between poverty and extravagance. I cannot pretend that all Victorians lived within their income; the Rawdon Crawleys would confute me if I did. But I think it is generally true that we are almost all, in the middle and upper classes at any rate, poorer than we were; and there is little doubt that we are more of us overdrawn at the bank. Another fact seems to me peculiarly symptomatic of what I call Chaos as against Cosmos. The Victorian public was seriously interested in the main work on which the nation was engaged. It respected Parliament; it read parliamentary debates; its newspapers were full of political matter and of serious argument. I suggest that the present-day public is not interested in the main affairs of the nation. Newspapers do not report the debates in Parliament. They give that space to crimes and betting news and interviews with passing celebrities such as cinema stars, athletes, pugilists, jockeys, dancers, and criminals. I am not raising any moral issue here. Nor am I forgetting that the England of the 'eighties wept hot tears over the departure of the elephant Jumbo from the Zoo to America. I only suggest that when a community as a whole is not interested in the great main issues which it itself has to decide, but turns aside to almost anything else as a diversion, that is a sign of Chaos as against Cosmos. In a Cosmos people give their minds to the main thing that they are doing. The main prizes of public life go to the real leaders, not to pugilists and cinema stars. One would not feel much confidence in an army in which the football champion or the man who sang funny songs was more admired and better paid than the General.

Some time ago I was in Paris during a by-election and was able to read the literature put out by the various candidates for the *arrondissement* in which I was staying. There were twelve of them; six at most would have been regarded as sane by a Victorian Englishman, four as, shall we say, "dotty", and two—a Fascist and a Communist—as obviously insane. After the first ballot all the reasonable candidates disappeared, the contest lay between the two madmen, and eventually the maddest got in. I do not for a moment give that incident as a proof of any great change; it is merely an illustration. The result—I was generally informed—did not at all represent the views of the majority of the voters; it represented the breakdown of political machinery and the general impotence of common sense. Chaos instead of Cosmos.

How did this breakdown come about? One thinks first of the direct action of the war. Of course, one must never forget the heroism and self-sacrifice demanded of the actual fighting soldier; but for the nation as a whole the effect of the long-continued war was to teach, not discipline, but indiscipline. In the first place, war is in its essence a formal repudiation of all social laws. Every weapon, every method, every form of violence and fraud, are legitimate for the sake of victory; inevitably, as the repugnance instinctively felt for such methods is once overcome, there grows up a tendency to use them not merely for victory in war, but for any purpose which is strongly desired. The ice is broken and people become familiar with strange doings. Again, when young men are facing danger and death for their country, great indulgence is felt for them. One forgives much licence, and even smiles at it. Inevitably the licence spreads to those who are not facing death. If Jack, the soldier, on his leave home, runs riot and is never criticized, why should not his brother Tom run riot equally? Why not his sister Jane?

In public life also war makes a change. Law is silent, custom is broken through, the constitution is set aside, the liberty of the individual is treated as a trifle. The objects of the war are won, not by reasonableness and fairness, not by scrupulous care to be in the right, and to do justice to your opponent—they are won by just the opposite qualities: by push, aggression, violence, ruthlessness and trickery, by always snatching the most you can and pressing every advantage, fair or foul. A generation largely brought up in such an atmosphere can hardly understand the deep respect for law and personal liberty, for reasonableness and fair play, for the ideal of citizenship and of honour, which is a natural growth in a peaceful and civilized society.

Education, of course, suffers. There is general loss of discipline among boys whose fathers and elder brothers are away at the war and even their mothers largely occupied away from home. The normal and healthy reaction of Youth against the authority of Age is intensified, partly by this, and still more by the killing off of an intermediate generation. The elder brother or the young uncle is in ordinary circumstances an interpreter between one generation and the next; but for the present age the elder brothers, uncles, and young fathers were mostly killed off, and the young left face to face with men forty and fifty years older.

One other strange influence of the war on public life must also be remembered. As it continued, as the first enthusiasm passed away, and too many young men were killed, as the propaganda became more and more extravagant and mendacious and its lies began to be found out, as the hardships and perhaps the brutalities of the fighting itself increased, there came a widespread loss of faith in the whole meaning and purpose of the war. Men were murdering each other, and apparently had to go on murdering each other— poor devils!—on both sides; but let no one insult their intelligence by telling them that it was all for noble objects. Their daily life in the army was beset by false pretences, "scrounges" and "wangles". Could they be sure that the whole war itself was not really a "wangle" of some kind, for the benefit of unknown brass-hats or politicians or financiers? And if those exalted persons could "wangle" and "profiteer" with men's blood, why should their victims not do the same? The blind cynicism produced by the war in many types of mind has been unforgettably described by C. E. Montague.

The sum-total of these various effects of the war period amounted to what is called a loss of standard. Every wholesome society has its own standards; and almost the whole *raison d'être* of a wise conservatism is to see that those standards are upheld. The daily conduct of human beings is seldom governed by appeals to their reason or to general principles; what moves them is the spell of their traditions and customs, and the expectations which their fellows have formed of them. A man is not often deterred from a course of action by the reflection that it is not in accordance with the Gospels or does not make for the greatest happiness of the greatest number; he will hesitate at once if he is reminded that it is not done, or not professional, or not decent. There is a kind of conduct that is expected of people, according to their profession or circumstances; and the expectation has a very strong binding force. It is just this standard of expectation that was temporarily broken down by the war. Those most affected ceased to care whether a thing was considered professional, or "good manners", or conduct befitting a gentleman. This rejection of conventions would, of course, be all to the good if in their stead were substituted some higher principle; but it is only a rare nature that will reject convention for the sake of Christian duty or the service of mankind. For the vast majority, when conventions go the things that take their place are Pleasure, Money, and Passion. By passion I mean some strong and immediate motive as contrasted with one that is high or remote; and it is the habit of acting on high and remote motives that builds up character. Furthermore, as long as people mainly behave as they are expected to behave, there is mutual confidence and trust. Trade is unhampered by suspicion, and representative institutions work. When the standard fails, you cannot trust your customer, your man of business, your elected representative. When Mussolini spoke of "trampling on the rotting corpse of Liberalism", he might almost as well have called it "the rotting corpse of conservatism or constitutionalism"; the thing that was rotting was the civilized pre-war society, based on representative institutions, normal expectations and mutual trust, murdered by the war and its satellites. To realize the extent to which this process has gone we should remind ourselves of the fate of parliamentary government throughout the world. The system which before the war was considered to be essential to civilization, at any rate if civilization was to advance, is now in peril of its life.

It has been overthrown in Italy, Spain, Poland, Lithuania, Serbia, and Russia, and we must not conceal from ourselves that even in the great parliamentary nations it is at present working ill. In France, at the time of the financial crisis, it almost ceased to operate: so many deputies continued, for the sake of winning their seats, to make pledges which they knew to be impossible of fulfilment. In Germany it has been almost impossible to form a government; the various groups were too much concerned with their party warfare to be able to co-operate for the good of the nation. In America the elections are felt to be more and more of a sham, and the issues between the two great parties less and less real. In England Parliament has not quite recovered its prestige after the degradation of the election in 1918: the parties of the Left are torn by faction; and a system of voting which is calculated to give power to a minority is deliberately continued. The war spirit, with its mistrust of fair dealing, its actual preference for a little spice of fraud and of violence in public life, is not yet extirpated, even in the traditional home of parliamentary government.

So much for the effects of the war: but we must not be misled. The war is not responsible for the whole change. The war only precipitated and misdirected a development which was bound to come in the natural course of progressive human history. Quite apart from the war there were other causes at work, calculated to break up the prosperous and established order of Nineteenth-Century England. There were economic causes: the gradual loss of Great Britain's industrial and commercial pre-eminence through the competition of larger nations, like America, and better educated nations, like Germany; the weakening of Great Britain in her great fortress, the coal trade, and the partial supersession of coal itself by oil, in which Great Britain has no great advantages, and by electricity based on water-power, where she is markedly weak. The price of wheat was rising, and industrial populations suffering in consequence. The invention of aircraft was destroying the value of Britain's insular position and imperilling her command of the sea. All these causes operating at a time when international co-operation and good will were vitally necessary to civilization, were spreading an atmosphere of bitter international competition and bitter class struggles at home. For in a falling market both capital and labour suffer, and each imputes its own suffering to the fault of the other. Meantime, of course, other inventions, such as the development of motor traffic, telephones and wireless, and other social conditions, such as the wider distribution of wealth among the working and shop-keeping classes, were in part at least counteracting these depressive tendencies, while in part they were hurrying on new social changes. In the main, I think, they tend towards a unifying of the nation; but I will not dwell upon the subject now.

Dissolvent agencies of an intellectual kind have been at work, not in one nation alone, but among the more educated classes throughout the world. The advance of science, or rather the sporadic advances made here and there over the whole realm of science, had largely upset the coherent cosmology, if I may use the term, of the generation of Huxley and Darwin. Not only were the advances very great—enough in themselves to be rather disturbing—they were also separate and unco-ordinated. No synthetic genius has yet arisen to enable us once more to see the world as a coherent whole. Evolution became less intelligible and less helpful to morals; more mechanical, as in Mendelism; more loose and mystical, as in Bergson and his followers. Curiously enough, I believe the increasing study of the insect world had a disturbing effect. Such advanced social systems based on such unimagined horrors made human morals seem like the make-believe ethics of the nursery. Above all, the whole conception of physics was, to a great extent, transformed. Matter disappeared, atoms were no longer indivisible, radiation seemed for a time at least to transmute something into nothing and to give an excuse for believing in miracles. Lorentz's transformation and Einstein's theory of relativity reduced physical events to formulæ which might be stated but—I here quote an extremely high authority—are not meant to be understood. The doctrine of gravitation, the very foundation of physical science, turned out to be only a formula, not a statement of fact, and not an entirely correct formula at that. The effect of this immense change in the scientific conception of the world has been, if I am not mistaken, to shake the general belief in science, therefore in knowledge, therefore in reason. Nothing was certain. Every supposed truth was overthrown. Life was a gamble. I have seen the facts about radiation seriously used as an argument for no longer questioning the miracle of the Gadarene swine: since the one story was not more surprising than the other! On the other hand, I have heard the discrediting of Victorian science used as a basis for discrediting Victorian morals. The fact is that a clear conception of the world as an intelligible, or apparently intelligible, whole is an immense influence towards regular and law-abiding conduct. Morality and decent living depend so much on the recognition of oneself as being only a member of a great ordered whole, not an isolated being whose sole purpose is its own happiness.

Let me dwell on this point for a moment. The very word "Cosmos" in the sense of world-order was created by the astronomical discoveries of the fourth century B.C. That age produced, I would suggest, a coherent and soul-satisfying view of the world on which the Western races of men have really been living ever since. By the discoveries of that age, so men believed, "the stars, which had always moved men's wonder and worship, were proved to be no wandering fires, but parts of an immense and apparently eternal order. One star might differ from another star in glory, but they were all alike in their obedience to law. The order or Cosmos of the heavens was a proven fact; therefore the Purpose of God was a proven fact; and though in its completeness inscrutable, it could at least in part be divined from the fact that all these varied and eternal splendours had for their centre our Earth and its ephemeral master, Man". Man was shown to be the central point of the universe, the focus of the loving purpose of God.[1]

This conception of astronomy lasted for two thousand years till it was overthrown by Copernicus. When Copernicus proved that, after all, the earth was not the centre, when later astronomers showed that the earth was a comparatively insignificant part of the solar system and our solar system itself only one among multitudes, the shock to the whole religious and moral system of thought was incalculable. If ever the mediæval Church neglected its opportunities, it was in not burning Copernicus. A world that is not anthropocentric is a world in which man does not vitally matter, and man's poor anthropomorphic conceptions of religion and morality, of divine "justice" or

[1] See *Five Stages of Greek Religion*, pp. 124 ff.

"benevolence" can hardly hope to be objectively valid. Sin has no effect whatever on the solar system. Nay, if we believe certain recent writers on physics, our whole conception of matter is helplessly subjective: not only such phrases as "attraction" and "repulsion" are mere anthropomorphic metaphors, but the same seems to be true of "matter", "time", and even "position". The physical world is not only non-moral, it is more alien from man than the human mind can conceive.[1] In reality the shock of the Copernican system was so great that, I would suggest, on the whole the human race has refused to pay any attention to it. We still act and feel as if the earth were the central star and the man the central being. The other conception was not only shocking; it was not comprehensible enough to form a basis of belief.

But, however that may be, there were discoveries in another realm which had a more shattering effect even than those in physics.

There was perhaps no subject in which the nineteenth century had made such great advances and discoveries as in the study of human character. If one takes scientific psychology, one might fairly say that the advance made between Bentham and William James was greater than that between

[1] See, for example, *Anthropomorphism and Physics*, by T. Percy Nunn, Hertz Lecture to the British Academy, 1926. I ought to add that, in my opinion, whatever bearing these arguments may have on a transcendental theory of ethics they do not touch a human theory. If sin has no effect on the solar system, neither has prussic acid; but it remains poisonous.

Aristotle and Bentham. If one takes the more synthetic and imaginative understanding of character which shows itself day by day in practical life but is registered most clearly in the novel, it is difficult to over-estimate the psychological gap between Fielding and Smollett on the one hand and George Eliot or Tolstoy on the other. We may observe, too, that the advance had a markedly Victorian character: it was an advance in sympathy, in imaginative understanding, in what the Greeks called *mimêsis* or artistic creation. The Victorian novelist knew his human beings as a dog-lover knows his dogs, not as a vivisectionist knows them. The knowledge as it spread enabled men to understand and get on with one another. Its effect on morals may be measured by the moral gap between the same groups of novelists; it made ideals higher and judgments more profound and more charitable.

But since then the vivisectionist in psychology has been at work. The discoveries made seem to be real; their value has often been proved in practical medicine. But they have not been co-ordinated, they have hardly been sifted and tested; in many respects they are incredible, in others terribly open to misunderstanding. Psychology is perhaps about where Chemistry was in the days of the Alchemists. I think the new discoveries will in course of time prove to be a great help to civilized mankind, both in the conduct of our own lives and in the judgments we form about others, but for the present there seems little doubt that the effect has been anarchical and destructive. Impulses hitherto regarded as unspeakably obscene or fantastically malignant and wicked have not only been recognized as real, but have received a quite disproportionate welcome from the public. What is almost worse, a number of activities which have hitherto been accounted noble or charitable or unselfish are now exposed as so many forms of common cruelty and sensuality and vanity masquerading in the plumes of fabulous virtues. I say "fabulous" because the old traditional ideals of humility, chastity, and unselfishness are by the new doctrines analysed away into mere psychological errors. As I said, I feel sure that in time this will right itself. The discovery of true facts must in the long run be helpful in dealing with life; but I do consider that for the time being the advent of psycho-analysis has had a most destructive effect on the cosmos of our moral ideas. It has made chaos if anything has.

There is one more element which must not be forgotten in estimating the change that has come over the educated classes in the present generation—that is, the increased emancipation and education of women. Again, I am convinced that the emancipation must in the long run be beneficial; the improved education is already enormously so. If anyone doubts it, I recommend him to visit a number of the new high schools and county secondary schools for girls throughout the country and compare, not merely the manners, but the general moral, imaginative, and intellectual influences existing in the schools with those prevalent in the homes from which most of the children come. The advance of about a century is being made in one generation. The increased freedom, as always happens, will be abused by the lower types, and will be a source of strength and good training to the higher. I see a good deal in newspapers and bad novels about the depravity of the modern young woman. And I can quite believe that a certain aimless and idle type of young person both behaves worse and is worse in a condition of freedom than when under strict mechanical control; but I can only say, and say with emphasis, that in my own limited experience, such as it is, I am constantly impressed by the high and strong character shown by the young and more or less emancipated women in the universities and in public work.

But the point which I wish to make is a simple one. We have here also an element of chaos. It will not be possible or desirable to impose on educated women who are earning their own livelihood in the world the same standards of manners and morals that were imposed on the women of Miss Austen or Dickens or Thackeray. One can expect far more of them: more vigour, more public spirit, more sincerity, more reasonableness. What degree of freedom they will demand in return will, I think, mainly be settled by themselves—not, of course, by the type that pursues cocktails and night clubs, but the type which seriously counts in the formation of character and of opinion. It cannot be doubted, and the subject cannot without some dishonesty be avoided, that great changes of opinion are taking place in the whole question of sexual morality. The Victorian standard has been shaken by the emancipation of women, by the discoveries in psychology, by the increasing importance and ever-widening practice of birth-control. Cosmos has been succeeded by chaos, and we must eventually find our Cosmos again.

What is the way? Curiously enough it is in international relations, the very spot where the nineteenth century showed its most fatal weakness, that we seem most conspicuously to have discovered the right method for rebuilding our ordered world. We have invented the League of Nations: before we fight we confer, and when conference gives no immediate answer, we convoke disinterested experts and set them to study the question. The League of Nations is in many ways a slow and comparatively weak instrument compared with, say, a national Parliament; but its essential method is perhaps wiser than that of Parliament. It is not content to vote down minorities. It works on and on till it wins their agreement. It almost never decides a question without real inquiry into the facts, and the inquiry is always made by disinterested persons, chosen for their special competence, and not dependent on Governments or popular votes. This last point is of cardinal importance. Governments can negotiate where their respective interests coincide or where both sides can drive a profitable bargain. Wherever there is real difficulty, where it is necessary either to take a wide view or a disinterested view or to look any considerable distance ahead, Governments are apt to be the worst negotiators possible. For normally every Government is possessed by a devil, the devil of the massed and organized selfishness of its nation. A Government can seldom afford to be generous or far-seeing in international negotiations, or the Opposition will accuse it of betraying the nation's interest to foreigners; and, as if the normal selfishness of human nature were not sturdy enough to be trusted, the nation will be urged by politicians and newspapers, first to formulate its extreme demands as just rights, and then—in mere love of righteousness—to insist on those just rights to the last inch. Almost every successful undertaking in recent international business has been first handled by disinterested experts, free from the clamour of national and party jealousies, and then passed on for Governmental approval when the hard brain-work was over. That is the regular League method.

There is one small organ of the League called the Committee of Intellectual Co-operation; but in reality Intellectual Co-operation is the characteristic instrument by which the League does most of its work. Say Austria is threatened with bankruptcy. How can she be rescued? Such an enterprise has never been undertaken before. However, a committee of financial and economic advisers is set to work. Punctilious care is taken that no private interest, and equally no national interest, shall affect the inquiry. A scientific and reasonable scheme is thought out, handed complete to the Council of the League, and so put into operation. If representatives of Governments had formed the committee, they would probably have spent all the time in fighting for small national advantages till there was no Austria left to save.—Say plague, typhus, malaria, and various epidemics are spreading through the world: the League selects the most suitable physicians it can find in its various states, adds others from Russia and America, and sets them to co-operate on the problem. They meet, they collect and compare evidence, and eventually devise a scheme for dealing with the epidemics, better and more effective than would have been dreamed of before the existence of the League. The Governments approve it; and, by the help of grants from the Rockefeller Foundation, the League puts it into effect.—Say that the currencies of most nations in Europe are breaking down, as they were in 1921; what is to be done? Call a conference of financial experts; let them show what is wrong and recommend remedies; let their report be recorded and published. Then, as soon as public opinion in the various states is calm enough to listen to reason, the Governments will carry out the advice. So it was hoped, and so in fact they have done.—Last year, again, to meet the dangerous stagnation of commerce, the falling off of sales and the increase of unemployment, the greatest effort of all was made. A great conference was called, not of Government representatives—for the Governments were all deeply pledged to the game of ruining one another—but of disinterested economists chosen or approved by the Governments of fifty-two states. If all the chief economists of the world thought out the problem together, and if a great majority recommended the same way out, it would be much easier for Governments to change their policy without losing votes. They did think it out together, and in their main recommendations they were unanimous. Unfortunately, the economic policy of most Governments is conducted by people with very little knowledge of economics, and subservient to a public opinion with almost none; but there before us is the advice, the unanimous advice, of the best economists of all civilized nations. Governments can follow it if they like, and European commerce will then, in all probability, be saved.

One could easily cite other cases. In all the principle has been the same. The first need is disinterested good will, the next is to pool the best brains of all nations for the common service of all. That is Intellectual Co-operation.[1]

The particular committee which bears the burden of that unattractive name has so far attacked chiefly some technical problems, concerned

---

[1] For the exposition of this idea see especially *Learning and Leadership*, by A. E. Zimmern, Assistant Director of the Institute of Intellectual Co-operation in Paris.

with the standardization of scientific terms, the preservation of documents, the co-ordination of bibliography for several sciences, the rights of authors, artists, and inventors, and the like, into which I need not enter. But its method is regularly the same: to convoke a committee of persons from different countries who know or care most about the subject in question, and set them to study it and make a report. Is there, or ought there to be, any property in scientific discovery, as there is in patents and copyright? If so, how can it best be assured with the least hindrance to industry? Can any method be found, without trenching on the independence of national systems of education, for making the rising generation throughout all the states of the League acquainted with the principles and practice of the League and familiar with the thought of international co-operation as the normal method of civilization? Let a sub-committee of educationists from different countries get to work on the problem and see what they suggest. As you know, they met and formed the scheme; the Assembly unanimously thought it a good scheme, and it is now being carried out. Last year the Committee laid the foundation of what may in the long run be an even greater work. It arranged a conference of the higher schools of International Politics, the institutions where in London, Paris, Berlin, and other capitals historians and publicists study the current international problems of the world. The conference took place; and will be succeeded

FROM CHAOS TO COSMOS

by others. And henceforth the expert political schools of Germany, France, England, Italy, and the other nations will be in regular touch with one another. A short time back such co-operation would have been contrary to all precedent. Knowledge would have been kept back. Both sides would have made avoidable mistakes. And in the last resort some difficult problem would have been doubly confounded by fighting instead of being solved by Intellectual Co-operation.

There is a story—a story whose historical veracity I must firmly decline to guarantee—about the foundation of the University of Buffalo, close by Niagara Falls. It relates that a group of wealthy and conscientious Americans looked at the millions of tons of water crashing over the Falls and considered what a terrific instrument of power was there for the hands of those who knew how to use it, what good it might do if used well and what harm if used wrongly. "We must have some first-rate electricians", they said, "to show how the power can be developed. We must have some experts on public health and town-planning and municipal government to show how it can best be used for public utility. We shall need an historian or two, to tell us if ever any community was in such a position before, and if so, what they did about it. We shall certainly need a Professor of Moral and Political Philosophy; and we shall hardly be safe without one or two clergymen to enable us to resist temptation." In the upshot, there was nothing for it but to found the whole University of Buffalo!

I feel that the world is at present confronted by not one but many Niagaras. How formidable and how often misdirected are the influences of the Press, the cinema, the wireless, the control of the air, the power of advertisement and of education; of powerful combines controlling monopolies or quasi-monopolies in such raw materials as oil and rubber, or even iron and coal! One can think of a dozen other forces, some of which have been mentioned in these lectures. Are these forces to be guided or not guided? Nay, guided they must be, if not by some effort of intelligence and good will, then by the stream of competitive money-making, by the struggles of the market, by the desire to cater for the widest and lowest taste, by the poison of antagonistic nationalisms, by the intrigues of interested parties, by the madness of armed conflict. Surely by now we know a better method. We have the instruments for practising it. Man has, in the last issue, only one weapon for dealing with the innumerable problems which bewilder and which may destroy him, the weapon of thought. Thought may go wrong; but it is the best guide we have, if it is patient, if it is based on study, if unwarped by personal interests and moved by the spirit of good will. Need we ask no more? Yes, just a little more. We may ask something of that spirit which, since the very beginnings of history, men have expected and found in the average common soldier—a will to endure hardship for the sake of duty and to use life as one who knows of things better than life.

That granted, I look to Intellectual Co-operation among men of good will for the restoring of our lost Cosmos and the ultimate wise guidance of the world.

THE BASIL HICKS LECTURE
DELIVERED TO THE UNIVERSITY OF SHEFFIELD
MARCH 8, 1928

THIS Lecture is included by kind permission of the Basil Hicks Foundation and of J. W. Northend, Ltd., of Sheffield, by whom it is separately published.

VII

THE SPECIAL PROBLEMS OF THE BRITISH EMPIRE IN RELATION TO THE LEAGUE OF NATIONS

PROPHECY has been described as a particularly gratuitous form of error. The existing world provides us with such ample opportunities of making mistakes that it seems unnecessary to seek out further ones in the world which does not yet exist. Yet the temptation is great. The historian Gibbon, after describing the fall of the Roman Empire in the West at the end of the fifth century, proceeds to discuss the possibility of a similar overthrow occurring to our modern civilization, an idea which often haunts the mind of a philosopher or historian. Gibbon decides firmly against it. Firstly, there are not nearly as many barbarians as there were. The civilized world has so vastly grown, and the barbarian proportionately decreased, in extent, numbers, population, and comparative power. Secondly, the Roman Empire suffered from too much centralization: when the centre went wrong the provinces were helpless. In the modern world, if the torch of civilization fell from the hands of one nation or continent, there would be others ready to carry it on. Gibbon foresaw the possibility of what our generation calls "The Yellow Peril", and he countered it by something like the League of Nations or Pan-Europa, aided, in the last resort, by a civilized

America. "If a savage conqueror should issue from the deserts of Tartary, he must repeatedly vanquish the robust peasants of Russia, the numerous armies of Germany, the gallant nobles of France, and the intrepid freemen of Britain, who might perhaps confederate for their common defence. Should the victorious barbarians carry slavery and desolation as far as the Atlantic Ocean, ten thousand vessels would transport beyond their pursuit the remains of civilized society; and Europe would revive and flourish in the American world." He proceeds, very acutely, to argue that North America will probably speak English, and then adds a remark which reads strangely at the present day: "Thirdly, the art of war has come to be itself so civilized." It is dependent on mathematics, chemistry, mechanics, and architecture: it is a slow and elaborate business, the defence being much stronger than the attack; and "the European forces are exercised by temperate and undecisive contests", which do little harm but serve to keep alive the manly spirit of the civilized peoples. In the meantime, he considered, the world was safe. "Every age has increased, and still increases, the real wealth, the happiness, the knowledge, and perhaps the virtue, of the human race."

This passage was published in 1781; before ten years were passed Europe was convulsed by the rising in France of an enemy of whom Gibbon had taken no account, the internal barbarian, the dispossessed and angry proletariat. Gibbon himself, like most of his class, was dazed by the

French Revolution. His letters show him passing through all the stages of panic. Such villains as the revolutionary leaders of France are sure to be rejected in a few weeks by the good sense of that polite nation; at any rate, they are the enemies of the human race, and no regard whatever must be paid to them or their ideas. "The slightest concession launches you without rudder or compass on a dark and dangerous ocean of theoretical experiment." (1792: cf. November 10, 1793.) Within twenty years the "temperate and undecisive contests" of European armies had become extremely intemperate and catastrophic; the attack had beaten the defence, and armies had begun to be numbered by hundreds instead of tens of thousands.

Gibbon completely overlooked the increasing destructiveness of war; yet his chief mistake, one might perhaps say, was to think too much in military terms, and not pay enough regard to the subtler forces of society and economics. The more recent Roman historians, such as Seeck and Rostovtzeff, attribute the fall of the Roman Empire much more to internal causes than to the attacks of foreign barbarians: the dying out of the cultured class, the bad economics, the impossible taxes, the decay of the roads, and the overwhelming influence of the most ignorant part of the population. This was largely due in the first instance to war, but not particularly to defeat in war. It was the continuance of war itself that was ruining and poisoning the world, and would have done so pretty much to the same degree whichever side won.

Gibbon, in 1781, wrote in a state of confident security. He lived to see that confidence shattered and society as a whole governed by a feeling of fear.

Insecurity is the note of the next forty or fifty years. Gibbon's terrified sentence declaring that no reform, however reasonable, was to be admitted, because a mad world would only demand its own ruin, represented the mind of the governing classes in most countries of Europe. I need not dwell on the oppressions of that period, in particular the crushing of all freedom of speech and thought. Then came a gradual release from fear; the Revolution and "Boney" ceased to be a constant obsession to men's minds. Europe, under the lead of Great Britain, was gradually launched on the wonderful career of hard-won reform and prosperity which marks the nineteenth century. If we take England alone, we find such advances as the abolition of slavery, the sweeping reform of the old criminal law and the penal system that accompanied it; the reform in the treatment of lunatics; the invention of anæsthetics; laws against cruelty to children and animals; the Factory Acts; the Married Woman's Property Acts; the immense spread of education; the beginnings of the care of public health; the greatly reduced consumption of alcohol. An enormous increase in the population was accompanied by a still greater increase in wealth per head. The state of the poor, bad to begin with and for some time growing worse, soon turned and began a steady career of shortening hours, improved conditions, and rising wages. The advance in science and material invention was something unparalleled in history, and was accompanied by a remarkable, if not quite an equal, harvest of art and literature. Security had returned in still greater measure, and with security an almost reckless freedom of thought and speech. The great imaginative writers of the nineteenth century liked to abuse their own age, and their contemporaries took the abuse smilingly, because they knew that it was not true and suspected it was meant as a joke or a paradox. The general tone was one of self-congratulation. Frederick Harrison hit off the age neatly when he compared it with that nobleman in Voltaire's story who possessed every virtue except modesty, and was presented by the King with a band of musicians who marched in front of him on all occasions singing:

> Que son mérite est extrême!
> Que de grâces! que de grandeur!
> Ah! combien monseigneur
> Doit être content de lui-même!

Mr. Marvin, in his brilliant little history of the civilization of the century, calls his book *The Century of Hope*. Mr. Brailsford, in the *War of Steel and Gold*, written in 1914, while denouncing the age in many ways, observes that it is not likely that there will ever again be a war between the Great Powers. Within three months the World

War had begun. The Century of Hope found its hopes blasted, and the period of security was over.

Let us dwell for a few moments on the characteristics of this period of security. In domestic affairs the feeling of confidence was based on a steady increase of all the elements that are conventionally held to make up prosperity. A critic might take almost any test of national welfare that he liked: population, wealth, tax-bearing capacity, education, literature, diminution of crime, naval and military strength, or the consumption of soap per head. On any reasonable test the age came out well. But perhaps there was no greater source of confidence than the fact that all this progress had come about together with, and apparently owing to, a steady increase of freedom. To make man prosperous and virtuous it seemed as if all that was necessary was to make him free. Strike off the shackles and the lame man will walk. Prosperity was not the result of ingenious governmental methods and long-thought-out artificial schemes; it was the result of natural causes, which operated as soon as they were given free play. And the reason why other nations were less prosperous than Great Britain was, generally speaking, because they were less free.

Consequently it was a time of extraordinary freedom of speech and thought. The age was so confident and had so clear a conscience that it rather liked to hear denunciations and paradoxes. The popular writers were mostly satirists. Thackeray satirized the ideals of the governing classes. Dickens laughed at almost every institution of the country; he gave us Jarndyce and Jarndyce, and the Circumlocution Office, and Bumble, and Gradgrind, and Pecksniff, and the government of the nation by Noodle, Boodle, and Foodle. One can feel that the laugh is good-natured, or at least that behind the satire there is a confidence that fundamentally all is well. When Carlyle thunders against respectability and explains the advantages of violence and lawlessness; when Tennyson inveighs against the corruptions of peace and clamours for "war, loud war by land and by sea"; when William Morris explains that the source of all wealth is robbing the poor; one recognizes everywhere an element of paradox. Like the hero of John Bull's Other Island, we say, "Reminds me of poor Ruskin; great man, you know", feeling that it is all nonsense, but no doubt does one good. In the generation after Dickens and Tennyson the satire and disbelief seem to cut deeper. There begins an incessant bombardment against the State, the Church, the Nonconformist Conscience, the middle class, and the institution of the family. If we look through Europe for writers who exercised a real intellectual influence during the later nineteenth century, and at the same time had a wide circulation in and beyond their own country, we should find, I think, some five names: Bernard Shaw, H. G. Wells, Tolstoy, Ibsen, and perhaps Anatole France —all of them rebels against convention, all children of the destroyer, whose flashing lights were welcomed and whose playing with fire was forgiven because their readers were imperturbably convinced that the house was fireproof. We were afraid of nothing in the 'eighties and 'nineties.

Far be it from me to speak disparagingly of these great writers, especially of Shaw and Tolstoy, to whom I personally owe so great a debt. They have certainly shaken the world from its dogmatic slumber. Anatole France, it may be, had no message except to destroy by ridicule piety and chastity—qualities which he apparently regarded as dangerously preponderant in Parisian society. My old friend Mr. Shaw, with all his clean intellect and his keen sense of pity, is certainly a Voltairian critic, a mocker, an iconoclast, a laughing genius who feels all the conventions of society to be absurd, and who shows their absurdity to millions of readers. Mr. Wells, with his gift for being interested in interesting things, and his wonderful powers of getting at once on to intimate terms with readers of every type, seems to me to preach a dangerous doctrine that we are none of us saints, none of us gentlemen, none of us chaste or sober or honest. John the Baptist might have said so much, but he would have commanded us to repent, which Mr. Wells never does. The rules of social morality, says a character in Ibsen, are "machine-stitched"; pick a little at one of them and the whole thing comes undone. The very word "Duty", says another, sounds like the cut of a whip. ("Duty" is *Pligt* in Norwegian.)

But the greatest, the most religious, and the

most destructive prophet of the nineteenth century was Tolstoy, as well as perhaps the greatest figure in its literature. Society to him was an orgy carried on by people who were permanently deluded and practically always drunk: "since a man who habitually smokes and drinks in moderation, in order to bring his brain into a normal condition, would require at least a week of abstinence from wine and tobacco. But this hardly ever occurs." It is more than an orgy; it is a fraud: "a fraud committed for the sake of those who are accustomed to live on the sweat and blood of others, who have perverted, and still pervert, Christ's teaching, which was given to man for his good, but has now become, in its perverted form, a chief source of human misery". Even more fundamentally anarchic is one of his defences of the doctrine of non-resistance to evil, in answer to the question how the doctrine could be carried out as a rule for society. "The question put by Christ is not at all 'Can non-resistance become a general law for humanity?' but 'How must each man act in order to do his allotted task and obey the will of God?'" This comes very near to saying, "Save your own soul and let an evil world perish".

Now, it seems to me that the civilized world in our generation has need of a quite different message. It is all very well to praise storms at sea when you are safe on land and not intending to make a voyage. It is all very well, like the writers I have mentioned, to ridicule the law and peace and conventional morality when you are not in danger of being left with no law and no peace and the standards of behaviour broken. But we of the present generation have walked too deep in the valley of the shadow. We have come too near to losing all that we value, and we see—if our eyes are open—too much danger still ahead. Our ship has got to be saved; saved with all its faults of construction and all its injustices, because only while it is safe shall we be able to correct the things that are wrong, reform the structure, improve the conditions of the cabin-boy, and bring ease to the starved and broken-legged cattle who are moaning in the hold. If we wish to be free, if we wish to be merciful, we must first see that civilization is safe.

Let us think first of the great society of which we are members and to which we owe our loyalty. We are a part of Western Civilization, the civilization built up by the thought and labour of many generations of great men—thinkers, artists, statesmen, leaders of their kind; we are a part, even more intimately, of the British Empire or Commonwealth. European Civilization perhaps is the whole fleet that must be saved; but the British Commonwealth is at least one of the greatest vessels, and the one to which you and I are allotted for service. There is fortunately no clash between the two loyalties; only the narrowest minds can imagine that there is. If European civilization goes, Great Britain goes; and if on the other hand Great Britain goes, it will be very difficult for European civilization to survive. And we must realize the fact that all the great Empires except our own have fallen: we stand alone, with the forces which destroyed the others largely concentrated against us.

Think for a moment of the strange position in which our great Commonwealth of Nations now stands. Before the war there was an Imperial Parliament and a Central Government with a great, though ill-defined, authority over all parts of the Empire. That has gone. The Imperial Conference of 1926 has laid down the absolute equality and independence of all the Dominions. The very phrase "Imperial Parliament" has been expunged. There is only a British Parliament exactly equal, but in no sense paramount, to the South African or Canadian. General Hertzog, formerly a professed Separatist, and confessing even now that he feels no particular love or reverence for Great Britain such as South Africans of British descent might feel, said: "I have been a lifelong opponent of imperialism and have feared the Empire, but as a result of the Imperial Conference the old Empire no longer exists. All that remains is a free alliance of Great Britain and six Dominions co-operating as friends.... The will binding us is our own will, and if to-morrow we want to get out of the Empire we shall go out."

General Smuts accepted Hertzog's statement as correct.[1] Mr. Bonar Law had said in the House of Commons a few years earlier (March 1920):

[1] Compare the interesting debates between Smuts and Hertzog in the South African Parliament in March 1928.

"The essential thing is that the Dominions have the control of their whole destinies. . . . If Australia or Canada chooses to-morrow to say, 'We will no longer form a part of the British Empire', we would not try to force them. Dominion Home Rule means the right to decide for themselves."

No doubt the instinct of British statesmen has been right. It may be that the Imperial Government showed a high generosity in resigning its claims: it may be that it merely recognized the limits of its power. In any case, it took the wise course. But that does not alter the fact that the developments of recent years have loosened the bonds of Empire throughout the whole multiform structure.

The protectorate over Egypt has been given up, though the impatience of Egyptian nationalists still delays the completion of the gift. Iraq is now only bound to us by a treaty, and will soon be an independent member of the League. Afghanistan has been relieved of her special obligations and is now the mistress of her own foreign policy. India is on her way to autonomy, and only hindering her own progress by that kind of excessive restiveness which arises from what psychologists call an inferiority complex.

The free Dominions have begun to assert their right to have separate representatives at foreign capitals; Canada and Ireland have already their Ministers at Washington and Paris. Canada has made a treaty with the U.S.A. about fisheries which, at her request, the British Government has not countersigned. And while the Dominions thus sign their own treaties, they have asserted their right to dissociate themselves from treaties signed by Great Britain. For example, they have not signed the Treaty of Lausanne. And Great Britain has fully accepted the position. In the several abortive treaties of alliance with France which were discussed between Lord Curzon and M. Poincaré there was always a clause explicitly excluding the Dominions from any responsibility. The same clause is actually embodied in the Treaty of Locarno. If Germany and France invade one another, Great Britain is bound to intervene at once, but Canada and Australia can look on unmoved. Or rather, to be quite exact, they are unmoved except for one consideration. They incur no active responsibility under the treaties; but since the King of England would, in the supposed case, be at war, and since Canada is one of his Dominions, the enemy would have a right to attack Canada if he chose so to increase the odds against himself and extend the range of the war. Canada thus incurs what is called a "passive responsibility". The risk is, in almost all conceivable cases, negligible. Yet, judging from my own few years of experience as a member of the Imperial Delegation at Geneva, I should say that the most serious anxiety that troubles the minds of the Dominions in the sphere of international relations is the fear of being somehow dragged into war again by Great Britain, as they were in 1914. Doubtless almost all the Dominions would rally to the defence of Great Britain if she were the victim of an aggressive attack; but even that would be an immense strain, and unless the rights of the case were beyond doubt and the interests of the Dominions more or less clearly involved, I think another war would probably be the end of the Empire.

But our position is in reality much more precarious than that single consideration would suggest. There are in the world as a whole certain well-known seeds of possible war or sources of discord; and it is curious to observe that practically all of these are to be found working inside the British Empire.

There is the possible war of colours; how long will the yellow or the brown races tolerate the absolute supremacy of the white? How long will even the black millions of Africa remain contentedly half-enslaved and at times gravely ill-treated, especially when the French have so obligingly taught them military drill and the use of modern weapons? There is the clash of civilizations—Christian, Moslem, and Oriental. There is the world problem of emigration and the distribution of population. How long will the overcrowded nations, like Japan, China, India, Italy, and perhaps Great Britain, contentedly remain choked with surplus population, while the owners of the vast empty territories all round the Pacific, such as Australia, Canada, and the U.S.A., deny —and for very weighty reasons deny—their people the right of entry?

If war should break out anywhere from one of

these causes, it is the British Empire that would be struck first, or almost first; if a war of colour, the Empire rules brown and black men by the million, and is more intimately involved with yellow China than any other European Power. She presents the contrast of white ruler and coloured subject on the greatest scale. If there is a war of civilizations, if Moslem ever rises against Christian, or Hindu against either, it is inside the Empire that the explosion will take place. If a war breaks out on the emigration question, the Empire contains to a high degree both the territories that demand emigration as a necessity of existence and the territories that will never admit immigrants. We are tied to the most dangerous of continents, Europe; to the most dangerous of oceans, the Pacific. We are interpenetrated by the most dangerous of subject civilizations, Islam. We are the chief representative of the most dangerous of international principles, the empire of one race of men over another. If only we have peace, secure and long-lasting peace, we can, I fully believe, by the spirit and machinery of the League of Nations, deal separately with all these tremendous problems and solve them one by one; but war would bring them all upon us at once and at a time when our hands were tied. The safety of the Empire, it seems to me, depends absolutely on the tranquillity of the world.[1]

---

[1] There are not many points of serious difference between the Home Government and any Dominion. We differ about the treatment of native races, especially in Africa. If we dared, we might reasonably object to the tariffs which some Dominions have put on

PROBLEMS OF BRITISH EMPIRE

Let us turn back to Gibbon and consider what are the main dangers which menace and may possibly overthrow that tranquillity. The first is Revolution. Nearly all the empires in the world have been already overthrown: the German, the Austrian, the Russian, the Turkish, the Chinese are gone; Japan and France are scarcely world-empires; the British world-empire stands alone. It is in some respects hardly any longer an empire, except in a few Crown Colonies. It is already freely spoken of as a Commonwealth rather than an Empire, but it stands firm, and has probably greater authority in the world than it had before the war. If we are shaken, all our rivals except the

with a special view to excluding British goods. There is always the possibility of a purely sentimental difference arising, like that about the Union Jack in South Africa; such disputes are apt to be dangerous because they do not yield to reason. As to the use of the King's veto, it clearly could not be subjected to any great strain. If the King's Ministers in some Dominion advised him to sign some Bill which his Ministers in another place advised him against, presumably he would delay signing till the next regular meeting of the Imperial Conference, or until some special conference could be got together.

And such dispute would be subjected, first, to all the peacemaking influences within the Empire, including those of the Privy Council and the Imperial Conference itself. Beyond that—supposing one of the disputants (e.g. Ireland or a Nationalist South Africa) felt irritable towards the Empire and the other Dominions, it would, as a last resort, be possible, by common agreement, to bring it before the League Council or the International Court. The League would, of course, have no right to interfere, but might be called in as an extra force for peace, supposing the forces within the Empire failed. Certainly the influences making for agreement would seem extremely strong.

It is interesting to notice that the only part of the Empire which has of late used anything approaching to a threat of war was not a self-governing Dominion, but a Crown Colony (Kenya), which was unwilling to treat its natives in a manner accordant with British traditions and the wishes of the Home Government.

U.S.A. have been worse shaken. And we must not forget that our Empire now has concentrated upon it almost all the discontent and the malignant propaganda that of old were more or less divided between the Kaiser, the Emperor Franz Josef, the Czar, Abdul Hamid, and others.

The Revolution that overthrew the various thrones of Europe seems to have stopped. Europe is fairly stable. The new Republics, though very democratic, are in many ways rather conservative than otherwise. The gigantic efforts made by the Russian Government to produce Bolshevik revolutions in Poland, the Baltic States, Rumania, Bulgaria, and, above all, Germany, may by now perhaps be said to have definitely and conclusively failed. The same effort has made almost no progress in India, and has been defeated for the time being even in China, where it seemed to have every circumstance in its favour. Over the rest of Asia it has successfully established itself. The Soviet system is a form of government, despotic, but based on the complete equality of all men—except the despots themselves—which suits the tradition and temper of undeveloped Asiatic tribes. And though theoretically Marxian and Communist, it appears that the Bolshevik leaders are not inclined to lay much stress on consistency where a non-industrial and non-communist system suits the circumstances better. Fortunately the low formless peasant civilization which now exists over the greater part of the Union of Soviet Socialist Republics seems to be incapable of anything like the organization required for an offensive war against any reasonably competent European state. The danger is of another kind.

Most civilized people to-day associate progress and peace in general with parliamentary or representative institutions. Some may think chiefly of the French principles of Liberty, Equality, Fraternity; others of the more modest British principle of government by consent rather than by force. The fundamental ideal is the same. Now, the curious thing has happened that in many parts of Europe, where parliamentary government has for some time been established and growing, it is at present weakening or breaking down, whereas in the East, where it is a strange exotic idea, it is being adopted with delirious excitement and combined with the heady wine of nationalism. Parliamentary government has been overthrown or shaken in Italy (40 millions), Spain (20), Poland (30), Lithuania (2), and Russia (120). In Russia and Turkey it came in the form of revolution, and was overthrown in its turn by a new and intensely nationalist despotism. Meanwhile it has spread into Persia, Afghanistan, Egypt, Iraq; has increased in India; and has passed through many wild vicissitudes amid the 400 millions of China. Now, parliamentary government has two aspects: it makes for peace and order when we think most of its method of peaceful voting and its principle that the minority loyally accept the wish of the majority; it makes for trouble when we think most of Parliament asserting its rights against kings or the small nations boldly defying the authority of the great. And, curiously enough, it is in Europe, where it made for agreement and order, that it has mostly been shaken, and in Asia, where it was associated with nationalism and the defiance of authority, that it has spread. The Asiatic movement is largely revolutionary and anti-European, or at least—since Britain is in Asia the great ruling Power—anti-British. There is cause for anxiety here, though not for alarm. Parliamentary government has behind it almost all the most civilized and most stable nations, and is besides indissolubly connected with the root principles of the League. Barring some strange accident, the League and civilization must win.

Nevertheless, a momentous conflict may well be brewing. Humanity is divided into many different races and colours: the white, the yellow, the brown, the red, and the black. And broadly speaking, with certain exceptions like the Turks and the Japanese, it is the white or Christian races that hold the empire of the world. They form the brain of the British Empire, they are all-powerful in the League of Nations, and they exercise over the other races a sort of recognized supremacy. There are three possible relations between the white races and the others: plain exploitation and virtual slavery, such as still exist in more places than one likes to think; nominal independence and equality, as in the U.S.A., a plausible ideal which breaks fatally down in practice; and the principle of Article XXII of the Covenant which makes the welfare and progress of the less advanced communities "a sacred trust of civilization". The phrase was a British phrase and drawn from the practice of the British Empire. The best white governors do carry out the "sacred trust", the worst fall back upon exploitation and virtual slavery. And it so happens that an utterly disproportionate amount of this "white-man's burden" has fallen upon the shoulders of the British Empire. Britain is the master everywhere; mostly, we like to believe, a good master; sometimes heroically good, in general fairly true to the principles of the Covenant. But the position of master is always an invidious one. There are abundant opportunities for misrepresentation; and some, of course, for well-grounded attack. And all the time, in every nation from China through Europe to the United States, a ceaseless militant propaganda, anti-Imperial and anti-British, anti-League, and mostly anti-Christian, backed by all the resources of one of the greatest nations of the world. The old Russian Empire did in diplomacy all it could against Great Britain; but it was so far in a weak position that as an alternative to British rule it could only offer Russian rule, and most people who saw the two unhesitatingly preferred the British. The present Russia has *prima facie* a far more attractive offer to make. In place of British rule it proposes absolute freedom for every nation.

The great advantage which Britain now possesses in this contest, as contrasted with the time before the war, is that through the League of Nations we can now, as long as our hands are clean, confute false statements and appeal to the public opinion of the world. This is a more effective weapon than most people realize. For example, the anti-British propaganda with regard to China has been practically killed, first by Sir Austen Chamberlain's action in laying all his information before the Council of the League, and secondly by the frank and convincing discussions of the unofficial but highly important Honolulu Conference. No such discussions were possible before the war. There was simply no means of laying the facts of any case before the Governments and Press of all the principal nations at the same time and inviting questions. International slander was the rule in all countries; and there was no method for killing it. Now there is. It can scarcely survive full public discussion before the Council or Assembly of the League.

It seems clear that, whatever may be the result of the various nationalist movements in Asia, the Communist propaganda in itself has failed. A war, a great economic disaster, any acute pressure of misery in the industrial nations, may change the situation; but, as far as one can judge from the present state of affairs, it seems safe to say that Europe will not become Communist and Southern Asia will not join the Soviet Republics. One might perhaps safely go farther and guess that a land like Russia, consisting almost entirely of peasants, with the town population weak and the intellectual upper classes non-existent, can hardly continue its nominal Marxian Communism, but must sooner or later settle down into a system of peasant proprietors. I think, therefore, that the danger of a world revolution is past, though there may be dangerous risings against the British Empire in Asia, and there will certainly be troublesome and wearing friction.

But the danger which Gibbon chiefly contemplated was war. He congratulated himself that the art of war has now become civilized and that "the European forces are exercised by temperate and indecisive contests" which do little but keep alive a manly spirit. He expected wars to continue, but had no conception of the magnitude they were going to reach. The great change in the situation is that whereas Gibbon only feared defeat in war, we have learned to fear war itself. As late as 1876 Disraeli could say: "We have no reason to fear war; Her Majesty has fleets and armies which are second to none." Only a madman could use such language to-day.

I think the increased deadliness of war is due principally to three causes. First, the great advance of nations in internal organization as well as in size. The Governments of France, Germany, and England learnt in the last war to do something that had never been done in the world before, to reach out their hands into every corner of their respective territories, so as to draw together and put into the field something like the whole strength of their people—of every man and woman as well as every factory and laboratory. The new French Act for the Organization of the Nation in time of War (March 1927) carries this process to the very limit of what is conceivable. Thus the power of mutual destruction possessed by two modern nations is something far vaster than was known in the past; and the exhaustion of both parties at the end of war is proportionately more complete.

Next, the immense international complexity of modern industrial and commercial life makes every disturbance of trade equilibrium more dangerous than it ever was before. Almost all the public troubles from which we are now suffering as a result of the war are due, not to death and destruction, but simply to disturbances of trade equilibrium.

One could take many instances; but the most striking, no doubt, is the dependence of Great Britain on oversea imports. In the Great War we were very nearly beaten by the German submarines, few in number and poor in quality as they were. Had Germany been as well provided with submarines at the beginning of the war as she was at the end, so my naval friends tell me, our necessary food supplies would have been stopped, Great Britain starved, and the Empire broken into its constituent parts. In Gibbon's England such interruption of imports would have been little more than a local inconvenience, as it would in Russia or China to-day. The old agricultural or pastoral communities could be cut in two and join again, as a worm joins. The modern industrial community receives the wound in a vital part and dies.

Thirdly, there is what one hears of most, the increased destructive power of weapons. I need hardly dwell on this. We all know that guns and shells are much larger, aeroplanes much faster and their bombs more widely devastating; poison gases far more numerous and deadly than they were at the end of the last war, though at that time they were far worse than at the beginning. We know, though few people seem to realize, that the Channel, which used to be the greatest of all national defences to this country, is now not a defence but a trap. The interval of sea is enough to imperil our supply of food and other necessaries; it is not enough to save our vital centres from attack. Two big guns on the other side of the Channel can make it impassable for ships; a good bomber can cross it in a quarter of an hour; and the only difference of opinion between air experts seems to be on the question how many tons of bombs would be necessary to destroy London and how many hours the destruction would take. Adequate defence seems—by most authorities—to be considered impossible. As Air Marshal Sir H. Trenchard has put it, "It is a misfortune for Great Britain that the air was ever invented"!

Sometimes the most extraordinary thing about modern humanity seems to be the power it has of recovery. It is impossible to calculate the destruction done by the last war or its increase in destructiveness over any previous war. Taking the material loss alone, one might compare the indemnity claimed from France after the war of 1870 with that demanded from Germany in 1919. The French in 1871 had to pay £200,000,000, and the world shuddered at the sum. The Germans, according to the first assessment of damage, had to pay £11,000,000,000; that is to say, fifty-five times as much. It was reduced afterwards to £6,600,000,000, which would be thirty-three times as much. The sum was reduced, and doubtless will be reduced further, not because it overestimates the material damage done, but because sums so vast cannot in practice be paid. Probably, so I am told, even the higher sum does not fully estimate the devastation suffered by the Allies; and, of course, in estimating the total damage done by the war, one must add that suffered by the enemy. In human life, the direct toll of war was over nine millions; the toll of disease and famine another ten millions; in maimed and damaged men it was incalculably more. I have not taken account of the indirect material losses. I have not touched at all on those deeper losses, imponderable and irrecoverable, of which it is best not to speak. The marvel is that we are still here to tell the tale. We have escaped, but only by a hairbreadth, if not by a miracle. Another time we can hardly hope to escape. Few thoughtful men will differ from the pronouncement of the Prime Minister:—

Who in Europe does not know that one more war in the West, and the civilization of the ages will fall with as great a shock as that of Rome?

Few will resist the conclusion of Lord Grey:—

We must learn or perish.

If these judgments are true, or even approximately true—and neither Mr. Baldwin nor Lord Grey is given to exaggeration—the central object of British policy must be not merely to jog along peacefully as it normally does, but by active foresight to exclude the possibility of war among the great civilized Powers. It is no good saying that we can let the nations of Europe fight if they want to fight, while we "keep out of it" ourselves. We are now united to Europe, as Lord Grey has put it, by "bonds as light as air and as strong as iron". If there is another great war in Europe, the United States may possibly keep out of it, but Great Britain will be drawn in. It is no good saying that one cause of war may be a British interest and another not; that we must defend the Rhine frontier but not some other frontier. The cause of war may not matter a scrap to us; what matters is the war itself. As Article XI of the Covenant frankly states, any war or threat of war is henceforth a danger to the whole civilized world.

Can war be abolished? Is it not rooted in human nature? Is not man a fighting animal? Or rather, is not strife an essential element in life itself? Such questions all miss the essential point. It is not proposed to abolish the struggle for existence, or angry passions, or any particular constituent of human nature; not even folly. It is proposed to abolish a certain method of political action which with the advance of civilization has become too expensive, too painful, too dangerous, and too futile. A modern war is not an outburst of passion. It is a carefully prepared and thought-out act of policy; and practically all the statesmen of Europe have now seen that it is a policy which does not pay, and have made agreements with a view to avoiding it. A modern war never breaks out from a blue sky. There are always disputes and moments of friction long beforehand; and now at the League of Nations these moments can generally be dealt with, and are dealt with, as they arise, long before they become dangerous. There is no change to be made in human nature, only a change in machinery and habits. And in these a vast change, much greater than most of us realize, has already begun. Where formerly an international conference was a rare and formidable affair, and every international agreement a precarious adventure liable to be wrecked by one dissentient, now the conferences take place as a matter of routine every three months, while settlements of disputes by arbitration or judicial settlement are so common and create so little concern that they are scarcely mentioned in the newspapers. How many of us realize that in the last seven years France, Germany, and Great Britain have all been before the International Court, all have lost cases as well as won them, none has complained, none has failed to obey the decision? Whereas formerly the Foreign Secretaries of the Great Powers never saw each other from the cradle to the grave, or at best might pay each other a solemn ceremonial visit, at which Europe trembled and journalists augured the worst, now they meet intimately, both in private and public, about every three months, and discuss the small clouds on the horizon like friends—and friends who do not mean to get wet. The change is profoundly significant.

The abolition of war among the civilized nations is not yet assured, but it is within human power. It is almost within reach. Not, of course, among the uncivilized; Pathans and Moors, Chinese tuchuns and Arabs, take their chief pride in fighting, and still in the main conduct the sort of war in which few people are killed and no great disturbance made in the social organism. War does not ruin those primitive societies; it is only the civilized industrial societies who are too rich to afford war. And one can see now, year by year and almost month by month, how the civilized nations are groping towards the abolition of it.

I remember in 1918, when I served on one of the advisory committees for drawing up the Covenant of the League of Nations, the question arose of putting into the Covenant some definite prohibition of war. And at that time it seemed too much to ask. It was essential to draw up a Covenant which nations in general would accept, and the committees dared not make the obligations too absolute. It was considered enough to insist that, before resorting to war, members of the League should agree to bring their disputes before the Council of the League, or some similar body, and at least allow their fellow-members full time to think out some proposal of peaceful settlement to which both sides might agree. No one could make them agree. They retained their liberty to go away and make war if they liked. The Covenant as it stands does, indeed, go one step farther. After prolonged and heated discussions it was agreed that if the rest of the Council or Assembly, apart from the disputants, is unanimous in its recommendation, the recommendation must be accepted by the disputants or at least not resisted by armed force. But if the Council is not unanimous, and no agreement is reached, then, after some nine months of waiting, the disputants are free to go to war.

That is the present situation under the Covenant. War is nearly excluded, but not quite. And ever since 1919 there has been a growing demand for excluding it altogether. The nations will not disarm while war still remains on the horizon. In 1924 every delegation in the Assembly accepted in first reading the famous Protocol. There were details in it which almost nobody liked, but it abolished war absolutely, and for that reason the anxious Governments accepted it. I shall never forget the enthusiasm with which the representatives of so many nations, some afflicted and suffering at the time, some victorious but fearful of the future, voted for that plan. The Protocol eventually failed, partly for irrelevant and accidental reasons, partly because of the too rigid and onerous obligations of mutual assistance which it imposed. But the statesmen of Europe have not given up their desire. Every year it is brought forward again. Baulked of the General Treaty for abolishing war, many pairs of nations have made separate treaties to that effect. The most important, of course, is the Treaty of Locarno between Germany and France and also between Germany and Belgium. It is not, strictly speaking, a treaty of "all-in" arbitration, but it is a treaty for the complete renunciation of war. Let me explain.

It is well known that disputes between nations are divided into justiciable and non-justiciable. The first are questions of fact, of law, of interpretation of a treaty, and of assessing damages, questions which are capable of definite legal decision; the others are mere clashes of interest in which there is no clear right or wrong. The first are suitable for definite decision by a Court; the others are more suitable for settlement by arrangement or compromise. An "all-in" arbitration treaty, in the strict sense, provides for the compulsory peaceful settlement of both kinds of dispute. Now, by the Treaty of Locarno the two parties first agree that all justiciable disputes between them shall be decided by the International Court. As for the other disputes, they set up an elaborate machinery of conciliation to try to find in each case an arrangement to which both sides can agree, but they do not in the last resort make the settlement compulsory. That still leaves the possibility—the remote possibility—that a dispute may not be settled. But it does not leave a possibility of war; for the second clause of the Treaty of Locarno runs:—

> Germany and Belgium, and also Germany and France, mutually undertake that they will in no case attack or invade each other or resort to war against each other.

In no case; except, of course, if the Treaty be broken. Not for points of honour, for there is no honour greater than keeping one's word: not for vital interests, for there is no interest so vital as peace. Not even in cases so evenly balanced that the Council fails to come to any decision; for, if the case is hard to unravel, it is better to leave it undecided for the time being; it would be better to decide it by the toss of a coin than by the competitive ruin of two peoples.

Locarno, I think, points the way. France, Germany, and Belgium have "outlawed" war between themselves. Similar treaties have been signed by Holland, Switzerland, Sweden, Italy: altogether, I believe, over seventy treaties of a similar character are in existence. M. Briand has made his celebrated offer to the United States of a treaty for the renunciation of war between the two nations; Mr. Kellogg has replied with his proposal for a general renunciation all round of "war as an instrument of national policy". I will not discuss the problems or difficulties attaching to each particular proposal. Enough has been said to show that there is a spirit in the world, not merely in pulpits and lecture-rooms, but in all the streets and workshops and Foreign Offices of Europe, which is seeking this way and that, at much sacrifice of national pride and sovereignty, for some agreement which will definitely banish and "outlaw" war beyond the horizon of the civilized world.

Great Britain, at Locarno, did not accept the same obligations to peace as France and Germany. But that does not, I hope, mean that either the nation or the Government is permanently unwilling to do so. Of course, there are certain reservations which may be necessitated by the peculiar position of the British Empire—though as a matter of fact every nation has some peculiar position of its own. Of course, we must consult the Dominions before taking so important a step. Of course, we must defend ourselves if attacked, and the rest of the League join in our defence. Of course, we must keep a fleet to police the seas against pirates and slave-traders, and an effective expeditionary force to defend our frontiers, in India and elsewhere, against savage neighbours. No nation is asking us to make any sacrifice of our interests or duties in these points. What the nations of Europe, as a whole, are asking us is a simple thing: to accept the same engagements against war which have been accepted by France and Germany. France and Germany have invited us. Holland has invited us; Switzerland has invited us; Sweden has invited us; but a certain section of diplomatic opinion in England steadily continues to refuse. We may go to arbitration, say these strange diplomats, but we must not promise beforehand to go to arbitration. We do not wish to go to war, but we must never promise not to go to war. We must keep our hands free! In God's name, free for what? Free to force on Europe that "one more war in the West" which, as the Prime Minister has assured us, will bring not only the British Empire, but "the civilization of the ages", down with a crash like that of Rome? If our hands are to be free for that, they will be tied for every wiser purpose.

They call it a policy of caution. It seems to me like caution run mad—a caution that is so afraid of certain minute dangers that it thinks, and actually speaks, of war as a "safety-valve".

It is not really a policy of caution. It is a survival from times when conditions were quite different; a remnant of eighteenth-century diplomacy which has somehow lingered on into our own day. I remember that the late head of the Foreign Office, Sir Eyre Crowe, used to argue against arbitration, at any rate for a great and strong nation like Great Britain. A strong nation in dispute with a weak nation, he would say, can generally impose its will. It need not go to war, it need scarcely even threaten war; as long as it keeps its hands free it can use diplomatic pressure to get its own way. If it accepts arbitration, it loses that power.

Yes, it loses the power to "use diplomatic pressure". It loses the power to threaten. It loses part of the unfair advantage which goes to the strong against the weak in a lawless society. But it gains instead the confidence of the world and the advantage of living in a society that is not lawless. It gains, by dropping a weapon which it can never dare to use, the enormous advantage of Security against Insecurity. For every civilized nation henceforth the first and most vital interest is to be free from the prospect of war, but most of all for the British Empire. We stand to gain nothing by war; we stand to lose all. We are of all the Powers of the Eastern hemisphere the richest, the most contented, and the most vulnerable.

I have argued my case to-day on grounds of material advantage and common prudence; perhaps you will say, almost by an appeal to fear. But at least not fear for ourselves; only for that stupendous heritage which is ours to protect and preserve. If it were necessary again, as in 1914, for men to risk their lives and women their happiness to preserve international good faith and free institutions, I should think, as I thought in 1914, that the sacrifice must be made. However peaceful the nations may become, man can never live a worthy life unless he holds it always as a soldier does, as a thing to be risked and, if need be, sacrificed in order to preserve something better than life. But the way to preserve civilization now is not to prepare for war, but to build boldly, with daring as well as prudence, a broad road to permanent and secure peace among the civilized nations. You will ask me what I mean by the civilized nations. Are they the nations that can build sixteen-inch guns and racing aeroplanes, or are they those which accept the rule of Law in the sphere of Law; in which large classes hold to some religion of Good Will and Justice, and believe, or try to believe, in something remotely resembling the Sermon on the Mount and the Thirteenth Chapter of Corinthians? You know, as a matter of plain fact, they are both. Through all the turmoil of dirt and injustice which seethes in the dark places of our modern civilization, it does in broad fact remain true that the power of wealth and force, the power to buy and to kill, does on the whole lie with those nations or groups of nations who are, I will not say worthy, but at any rate the least unworthy, to hold that tremendous trust. It is a serious thing for a man to be another man's master. Much more serious for a nation to be master of another nation. But clearly it is better for the world to be led by the civilized man than by the savage, provided only that the civilized man is true to his own civilization.

Inasmuch as we are really higher than the savage, let us remember what principles and what kinds of men have made us so. Not the cynics and conquerors and so-called empire-builders; not the heroes of violence or cunning or avarice. The savage has all the feelings and ideas that those men have; there is little difference between him and them except the difference of wealth and opportunity. It is the soldiers who have thought more of protecting the weak than of gaining glory; the traders whose word is as their bond. It is the saints and thinkers, the artists and poets and men of science, the millions of decent kindly men and women who have done faithfully their daily duties, and whose words or deeds have lived on, shaping those who knew them towards a life different from that of the savage; gentler, cleaner, more reasonable, more alive to beauty, more careful of the welfare of others, and more penetrated by the things of the spirit. By acting on the principles of that civilization we must inevitably move towards the abolition of war among the nations who share in it, and only by the abolition of war can our civilization be saved.

For Product Safety Concerns and Information please contact our EU representative GPSR@taylorandfrancis.com
Taylor & Francis Verlag GmbH, Kaufingerstraße 24, 80331 München, Germany

www.ingramcontent.com/pod-product-compliance
Lightning Source LLC
Chambersburg PA
CBHW050630300426
44112CB00012B/1742